www.ingramcontent.com/pod-product-compliance
Lightning Source LLC
Chambersburg PA
CBHW081109170526
45165CB00008B/2386

Thank You For Reading This Book.

10,000+ Selling Words & Phrases

From A to Z

By: Randall Kowalenko

LEGAL NOTICE

Table of Contents

Dedication

This book is dedicated to you & your copywriting success!

For God so loved the world that he gave his one and only Son, that whoever believes in him shall not perish but have eternal life. John 3:16 (NIV)

Please visit **www.NeedHim.org** for more information about salvation today!

Forward

Copywriting is a great skill that can have profound effects on your sales conversion rates when employed properly.

This book can help you by providing you with words and phrases that can aide your sales writing efforts. If you are having a case of writers block it's likely that a quick browse through this text can not only get your creative juices flowing again, but will likely offer a multitude of wording solutions to choose from.

Whether you are a new beginner or an advanced veteran in your pursuit of copywriting success this publication can offer you an arsenal of sales words & phrases to assist in your writing endeavors - both small and large.

I trust the information presented within will be very provocative to help you find creative word options when writing - especially when you are at a loss for words, are stuck, or even if you want to jazz up your sales lingo.

It is with great honor that I provide this resource to you and look forward to your copywriting success!

Randall Kowalenko

How To Use This Book

Organization of so many words and phrases is no easy task. As a result, the book has been arranged with a couple of avenues to help aide in your research efforts:

- The words and phrases are listed in alphabetized chapters

- Words can also be found by using the exhaustive index in the back of the book, which will tell you every page you can find specific words which may be included in phrases throughout this book

This book format is a great way which you can quickly identify, discover and uncover words and phrases quickly.

Words & Phrases
That Start With A Dollar
Amount

$ a month or more
$ a year or more
$ every single month
$ from my bedroom
$ grand
$ in free advertising
$ in free publicity
$ worth of
$ worth of bonuses
$ worth of merchandise
$ per click through
$ per lead
$ per sale

Words & Phrases
That Start With A Number

(no) affiliate sales will pay for it
(no) cents
(no) characteristics of
(no) customers in (no) day(s)
(no) day free trial
(no) day trial pass
(no) days free access
(no) different
(no) different ways
(no) easy payments of
(no) elements you can
(no) examples
(no) feet
(no) figure income
(no) foot
(no) free bonuses worth $
(no) freebies valued at $
(no) friends of mine
(no) full years of
(no) gallon
(no) grams
(no) helpful links
(no) hits in less than (no) hour(s)
(no) hot reasons
(no) information packed pages
(no) information rich chapters
(no) items you
(no) karat
(no) key principles you
(no) key questions
(no) kinds of
(no) knowledge packed lessons
(no) leads in (no) week(s)
(no) lesson course
(no) mistakes that
(no) months ago
(no) out of every (no)
(no) piece
(no) piece collection

(no) places to
(no) pounds
(no) proven strategies
(no) quart
(no) quarters
(no) resources
(no) rules you must
(no) sales in (no) month(s)
(no) sales will pay for it
(no) sections on
(no) simple formulas
(no) step system
(no) strong
(no) subscribers
(no) things to consider
(no) tips and tricks
(no) types of
(no) ways to
(no) ways to use our product
(no) year subscription
(no) years ago
(no) years in the making
(no) years later in (year)
(no)% commission
(no)inches
(no)piece
(no)th century

Words & Phrases
That Start With A Product
Name or Source

(product name) includes
(product / product name)) contains
(source) felt
(source) has/have proven
(source) heard
(source) said it look like
(source) saw
(source) says
(source) says it sounds
(source) stated
(source) studies show
(source) surveys show
(source) tests show
(source) thinks
(source) told me

Words & Phrases
That Start With A
Percentage or Number

100% of every sale
100% original information
100% pure traffic
100% royalty free resell rights
2 tier
24 hours a day, 7 days a week
24/7 affiliate support
24/7 presence
24/7 service
24/7 support
50-50 proposition
6 figure income
6 figures each year
9 to 5

Words & Phrases That Start With
"A"

a (no) minute
a (year) classic
a absolute must
a balanced life
a blueprint for
a booming business
a breath of fresh air
a breeze
a brief list of
a brief summary of what's
a chance like no other
a child could do it
a cinch
a collection of
a complete
a complete arsenal of
a complete package
a copy of my deposit
a couple hours a week
a custom designed
a cut above the rest
a date with destiny
a detailed
a diamond in the rough
a dime a dozen
a dirt cheap way
a drop in the bucket
a few of the features
a few success stories
a fortune this year
a free & easy way to
a fresh approach
a full (no) day guarantee
a full archive of
a glimpse of my sales
a gold mine of information
a good friend of mine
a great addition
a guaranteed gain

a guide to
a high degree of
a huge collection of
a letter from a client
a list of
a list of all
a long shot
a long story made short
a long time coming
a lot of people feel that
a massive collection of
a must read
a new lease on life
a new perspective
a new twist
a no brainer
a non stop salesman
a novel twist
a numbers game
a partial list of what
a place you can go
a pretty penny
a professional image
a proven blueprint
a quick fix
a revised and expanded
a rich source
a secret that
a secret weapon
a short list of our clients
a short list of what
a sign of the times
a simple
a simple technique that
a simple test to
a small list of
a small portion of
a snap
a special arrangement

a step forward
a study conducted by
a summary of everything included
a sure thing
a valuable reference
a way to get
a wealth of information
able minded
abnormal
above and beyond
above average income
above ground
above normal
abreast of changing regulations
abridged version
abrupt ending
absolute fact
absolute influence
absolute necessity
absolute power
absolute reason
absolute standards
absolute
absorbable
absorbing
absorbing story
abstracted from
abundant in
academic background in
academic like
academy like
accelerate your
accelerated
accented with
accept credit cards in minutes
accept your offers
accept your proposal
accepted business practices
accepted by

access proof
access time
access to all past issues
accessible
accessories included
accident prone
accidental
acclaimed
accompanied by
accomplish your
accomplished
accomplishing a goal
according to
accountability
accountable
accountant like
accounted for
accuracy and precision
accuracy tested
accurate information
accurate methods
accurate records
accused of
ace in the hole
achieve goals
achieve instant credibility
achieve the success you deserve
achieve top rankings
achieve your
achieving success
acknowledged by
acknowledged expert
acknowledged forerunner
acknowledgment
acquire your
acquired taste
acrobatic
act now
act upon

act upon your suggestions
act within (hour, days, etc.)
activate your
activated by
activation fee
active company
active market
active participation
actor like
actress like
actual case studies
actual people
ad claims
ad like
adapt to
adaptable
adaptive
add another income
add emotional value
add on
add on business
add on products
add up
add your
add your own links
added bonus
addict like
addicted
addiction free
addictive
additional
additional benefits
additional income
additional stream of income
additive free
address your
addressed by
adequate insurance
adhered to

adhesive like
adjoin at
adjust your
adjusted
administer
administrated by
administrator
admirable
admirer the
admissible in
admit that
adoptive
adorable
adore the
adrenaline rush
adsorbing
adult
advance
advanced
advanced equipment
advanced formula
advantage
advantageous features
adventure
adverse reaction
advertise
advertise to millions
advertise to thousands
advertised
advertisement free
advertising allowance
advertising impressions
advertising related
advertising space
advertising strategy
advice from
advice jammed
advisable
advise your

advised by

advocated to

aerial

affected by

affection prone

affectionate

affiliate

affiliate bonus

affiliate contests

affiliate discounts

affiliate newsletter

affiliate program

affiliate selling

affiliation

affirm your

affirmations

affirmative

affix your

affluent in

affluent times

afford luxury items

afford the

affordable

affordable accommodations

affordable price

afraid of

after hours

after tax

after years of

against the wall

age old

agenda

agent runned

agony free

agree that

agreed to

agreement

ahead of

ahead of the game

ahead of the pack

aided by

aim at

aiming for

air conditioned

air cooled

air heating

air like

air proof

air sealed

air tight

airborne

alarmed that

alarming

alarming increase

alarming speed

alien like

alien proof

alienated by

aligned

alignment free

alive and kicking

all about

all absorbing

all consuming

all day

all embracing

all female

all I can say is

all important

all in one place

all inclusive

all male

all natural

all night

all of the resources

all or nothing

all powerful

all purpose

all round
all star
all systems go
all terrain
all the ( ) you'll need
all the business you want
all the ins and outs
all the tools you will need
all the way
all time record
all walks of life
all washed up
all you do is advertise
all you need to know
allergy free
alliance with
allocated by
allow yourself
allowance
allowed to
alluring terrain
almighty
almighty dollar
almost controversial
almost everyone has heard of
almost perfect
almost too good to be true
altar your
altered by
alternated
alternating
alternative strategies
always adding new products
amazed
amazement
amazing
amazing ability
amazing advertising tips
amazing amount

amazing collection
amazing discovery
amazing features
amazing improvement
amazing results
amazing scene
amazingly effective
amazingly simple
ambition seeking
ambitious
ambitious growth
amended
ammunition filled
amount to something
amphibious
amplified
amplify
amplify your orders
amusement
amusing
an absolute winner
an action plan for
an angel
an arm and leg
an astronomical living
an email from a customer
an extra surprise
an idea whose time has
an in depth look
an instant business
an Internet fortune
an offer you can't refuse
an old age problem
analysis
analysis of
analyzed
ancestor
ancestral
ancestry

anchor down
ancient
ancient myth
ancient secrets
ancient truth
angel like
anger free
angered by
angled
anguish free
animal like
animated like
ankle deep
anniversary
annoyance free
annoyed by
annoying
annual earnings
annual sale
anonymous
answerable
answered by
answering your questions
answers hundreds of your questions
anti drug
anti virus
anticipated by
antique
any budget
any CEO will agree
anybody
anyhow
anyone
anyone can do it
anyone who buys will
anyone who is serious about
anyplace
anything
anytime

anyway
anywhere
apart from
apologetic
apology
apparent advantage
appeal to prospects
appealing
appealing alternative
appealing choice
appealing fragrance
appearance friendly
appliance like
applicable
application required
appointed by
appraisal proof
appraised by
appreciate by
apprentice friendly
approachable
appropriate
appropriate alternative
approval rating
approved by
approximat value of
archive your goals
are you a ( ) who has been trying to
are you looking
are you looking for
are you ready to
are you serious about
are...?
arm raising
arm twisting
armed with
around the clock
around the clock service
arousing

arranged by
array of colors
art like
article mentioned
artifact
artificial
artist signed
as good as it gets
as heard on
as mentioned on
as seen in
as seen on
as soon as possible
ask yourself
ask yourself this question
asking price
assassin proof
assembled by
assembles fast
assembly less
assert yourself
assess your
assessable to
assessed by
asset
assigned to
assists you
associate
associate program
association
assumable
assume your
assumed by many
assure yourself of
assured by
astonishing
astonishing ability
astonishing size
astounding

astounding ability
astounding collection
astounding efficiency
astounding miracle
astounding power
astronomical proportions
astronomical sales
at a premium
at the age of (no) I
at your fingertips
athlete like
athletic
athletic looking
atomic
attachments
attain celebrity status
attainable
attempt to
attend today
attention driven
attention grabbing
attentive service
attest to
attitude adjuster
attract customers
attract new clients
attract prospects
attracting business
attractive
attractive deal
attractive incentive
attractive investment
attractive price
auction like
audible
audio
audit proof
augmented
authentic

authentic antique
authentic flavor
authentic miracle
authentication
author of
authored by
authoring
authoritative
authoritative reports
authority on
authorization require
authorized by
authorized version
auto pilot
auto pilot income stream
auto saved
autographed
automate
automate everything
automate your follow up
automate your product fulfillment
automate your prospecting
automate your site
automated
automated income
automated profit generators
automated tools
automatic
automatic marketing system
automatic merchandising
automatic sponsoring
automatically deposited in your bank
automatically submit
automating
automation
autosuggestibility
availability limited
available
available funding

available in hard copy format
avalanche of sales
average
average sized
avid fan of
avoid costly mistakes
avoid mistakes
avoid pain
avoid problems
avoid the big mistakes
avoid the costly mistakes
avoid the costly pitfalls
avoid the run around
award winning
award winning presentation
awarded
awe inspiring
awe struck
awed
awesome
awesome pay plans
awesome size
awful looking
awhile back I

Words & Phrases That Start With "B"

babe magnet
baby like
back alley
back breaking
back end
back end profits
back handing
back in the saddle
back order
back when I was just
backdoor selling
backed by
background
backlash
backlogged
backed up
bad
bad debt
bad economy
bag like
bag of tricks
bags of cash
bail out
balance your
balanced
bald like
ball and chain
ball park figure
ballistic
balloon your business
band like
bang
bank like
bankable
bankrolled
bankrupt proof
bankruptcy
banned
banner like

banner year
bar like
barbecued
bare
bare basics
bare boned
bare truth
barely
barely scratched the surface
bargain
bargain conscious
bargain hunter
bargain price
bargained
barn burner
barrier proof
barring out
barter deal
base line
base on a true story
based in
based on
based on my experiences
basic
basic advice
basic guide
basic survival
basically you
basics of
basket full
bastard like
battered
battery powered
battle hardened
battle tested
be a major player
be a super affiliate
be an affiliate
be an expert

be completely satisfied or
be one of the first
be rich and successful
be selling in minutes
be your own boss
beach like
beached
bearable
beast like
beat competition
beat recession
beatable
beaten
beating the competition
beautiful
beautiful scenery
beautifully
beauty
because you
become a bona fide expert
become a expert
become a millionaire
become a paid subscriber
become a pro
become a super associate
become an expert in your field
become profitable
become rich
beef up
been publishing since
been well kept
before I share with you
beg you
begging
begin by
begin profiting now
begin without any
beginner
beginner to advanced

behind closed doors
behind the scenes
behind the scenes look
being a leader
being an expert
being educated
being famous
being in first place
being informative
being intelligent
being organized
being successful
belief driven
believability
believable
believably
believe
believe us or not
belly buster
belong to
belonging
belonging to a certain group
below average
below is proof that
below market
bend the rules
beneath you
beneficial
beneficial advice
beneficial agreement
beneficial influence
beneficial ties
beneficiary
benefit
benefits
benefits you'll get
bent over
berry flavored
beside yourself

best
best $ I every spent
best home businesses
best investment I've ever made
best is yet to come
best kept secret
best managed companies
best money can buy
best money I have ever spent
best price points
best promotional tools
best selection
best seller
best selling
best shot
beta test
beta test offer
beta version
better late than never
better paying
better than
between success and failure
beware of
bewildering
bewilderment
bewitched
beyond expectations
beyond your wildest dreams
bible like
big
big and bold
big breakthrough
big business
big check
big company
big corporation
big deal
big enough
big hearted

big hitter
big issue
big name
big reduction
big residual checks
big spender
big stacks of money
big ticket item
big time
big time operator
big trends
big wig
biggest
billed to
billing cycle
billing defrred
billion dollar company
billion dollar empire
billion dollar industry
billionaire
billions
binary plan
bind together
binding
binding commitment
binding promise
birth date
birthday
birthplace
bite sized
bitter sweet
bizarre
bizarre tactics
bizarre twist
black and white
black colored
black market
blast off
blatant

blazing
bleak chances
blended
bless
blessed
blessing
blew up
blind like
blistering speed
blizzard like
blockbuster
blocked
blonde
blood
blood and guts
blood red
blood stained
blood thirsty
bloody
blossoming
blow
blow by blow
blow it wide open
blow the lid off of
blow the whistle
blow up
blow up your profits
blown apart
blown away
blown out
blue collar
blue colored
blue ribbon
blueprint
blueprint for
board of directors
bodacious
bodily harm
body sculpting

boggle your
boil over
boiled
bold
bold look
bold offer
boldly
bolt out
bomb like
bombard
bona fide
bonded by
bonding
bone chilling
bone dry
bone jarring
bonkers over
bonus
bonuses
book like
book value
booked
booked months ahead
boom
booming
booming industry
booming trade
boost
boost sales
boost your
boost your response
boost your response rates
borderline
born again
born and raised
born on
bottled
bottom
bottom line

bottoming
bottomless
bounce back
bounce less
bouncy
bound and determined
bound up
boundary line
boxed
brace yourself
braced by
braided
brain burned
brain friendly
brainy
brand
brand image
brand loyalty
brand name
brand new
brand positioning
branded
branding
branding solution
brass
brat like
bratty
brave
breach of
bread and butter
break
break a leg
break away
break down
break even
break free from
break in
break new ground
break out

break out of your
break the bank
break the ice
break up
breakable
breaking news
breakneck speed
breakthrough
breakthrough discovery
breathtaking
breathtaking display
breathtaking picture
breathtaking scene
breathtaking view
breezy
bribe proof
bricks and mortar
brief
bright
bright colors
bright eye
bright future
brightly colored
brightness
brilliant
brilliant color
bring home the bacon
bring in
brink of
brisk
brittle
broad
broad base support
broad experience
broad minded
broad spectrum
broadened
broke
broken

broker friendly
bronze like
brought in over $
brown colored
browse around
brutally honest
bubble less
bubble wrapped
buckle down
buckled
buddy buddy
buddy like
budget
budgeted
buffed
bug like
bugged by
build a client base
build a global network
build an empire
build business relationships
build consumer trust
build profitable alliances
build self confidence
build strategic alliances
build your
build your business
building block
built
built in
built in affiliate program
built in business
built like a
built to order
built up
bulk of
bull headed
bullet proof
bullet proof system

bullet stopping
bull's eye
bully proof
bum rap
bumpy
bunched together
bundles of cash
bureau of
burglar proof
burn rubber
burned by
burning desire
burning issue
burning question
burst of cash
bury the hatched
business
business alliance
business as usual
business building
business consulting
business equipment
business from referrals
business geniuses
business information
business law
business leads
business letter
business like
business machinery
business model
business name
business needs
business owner
business partner
business plan
business planning help
business relationships
business secrets

business seminar
business vehicles
business venture
business veteran
business wants
bust onto the scene
busted by
busy
busy time
butt kicking
buy
buy a better car
buy a bigger house
buy a new car
buy a new house
buy again and again
buy anything from you
buy before midnight tonight
buy it already
buy now
buy on impulse
buy over and over
buyer behavior
buying power
buying whatever they want
by leaps and bounds
by the book
by the numbers
by the truckfull
bypass

Words & Phrases That Start With
"C"

cajole
cakewalk
calculate your order
calculated
caliber
call it like you see it
call now
call the shots
call toll free
call your own shots
camera ready
camouflaged
can be digitally download
can I show you
can you
can you handle
cancel anytime
canceled on
candy like
canned
can't imagine a better investment
can't live without it
can't match the sheer potential
can't put it into words
can't you
capable of
capitalize on
captivating results
capture customers
capture interested prospects
carbonated
career improving
carefree living
careful inspected
careful supervision
carefully selected
caring
caring service
carnival like

carries a lot of weight
carry out
carry the torch
cartoon like
carve out a niche
carved in stone
case by case
case history
case in point
case sensitive
case study
cases studies
cash
cash at closing
cash back
cash bearing
cash cow
cash discount
cash flow
cash generating
cash grants
cash in
cash in on
cash in on your share
cash in your chips
cash in your pocket
cash incentive
cash instantly deposited
cash magnet
cash on delivery
cash on demand
cash or credit
cash paying customers
cash rebate
cash secrets
cash starved
cash value
casino like
casual

cat and mouse
cat like
cataloged
catapult your sales
catastrophic results
catch 22
catchy
categorized by
causal
caution
cautionary
celebrated by many
celebrity status
cemented
center
centered
centralized
centuries old
centuries owned
ceramic
certifiable
certified by
chairman
chairman of the board
chalk up your
challenged by
challenging
chamber of
champion of
chance of a lifetime
change their beliefs
change their mind
change your destiny
change your life
changeable
changed forever
changed my life
channels of distribution
chapter (no) will show you

chapter (no) you'll uncover
charge it
charge the right price
charity giving
charmer
charming
charming beauty
charming hospitality
chat with us
cheap
cheap imitation
cheapskate
cheat proof
check in
check out these comments
checked
checked out what others
checklist of
checkout
checks in your mailbox
cheerful help
chemical free
cherish by many
child like
child proof
chill out
chilled
chilly
chipped
chock full of
chocolate covered
choose your own schedule
choosing the right
chopped
chosen by many
chrome
chronologically
chunky
cinnamon flavored

circle	clear solution
circle the wagons	clear thinking
circular	clear understanding
circulated by	cleared
circulation of	clearinghouse
circus like	clearly defined
citrus	clearly explained
city like	clearly written
city smart	clever
claimed by many	clever advice
clarified it with	clever devise
classed alone	clever ideas
classic	clever scheme
classic style	clever tactics
classifiable	cleverly designed
classification	click here
classified	client attracting
classified information	client driven
classy	climate safe
clean	climb on the bandwagon
clean bill	climbable
clean cut	clinical evidence
clean the floor	clock like
clean up	clocked at
cleanest	clockwork
cleansing	clone your sales
clear communicator	close at hand
clear cut	close deals effectively
clear cut answers	close every sale
clear cut proposal	close fitting
clear cut report	close in
clear examples	close knit
clear eyed	close out
clear headed	close sales faster
clear ideas	close supervision
clear language	close the deal
clear policy	close the sale
clear proof	close ties
clear sighted	close up

closed door
closely guarded strategies
closely monitors
closes at (time)
closing down soon
closing forever
club like
coached by
coaching included
coast to coast
coastal
coated with
co-author
co-authored
coded
coefficient
coffin like
coiled
coin operated
cold
cold blooded
cold cash
cold hard facts
cold hearted
cold shoulder
cold sweat
cold turkey
colder
coldest
collaborated with
collateral free
collect them all
collectable
collected by
collectible
collector's edition
collector's item
college like
collision proof

colonial
color
color organized
colorable
colorful
colorful demonstration
colossal amount
colossal wealth
combination locked
combined with
combustible
combustible issue
come and go
come full circle
come on strong
come out ahead
come out on top
come out swinging
come to a head
come to grips with
come to terms with
come up with
comeback to
comes with free reseller program
comes with the territory
comfort
comfort of home
comfort zone
comfortable
comfortable accommodations
comfortable fit
comforting
comical
commendable
comments from satisfied customers
commerce friendly
commercial
commercially sold
commission check

commission on back end sales
commission on repeat sales
commissioned by
commitment to
committed to
common cause
common in most
common purpose
commonsense to buy
commonwealth
communication oriented
community oriented
compact
companionable
company loyal
company stock
comparable to
comparative
compare it with other opportunities
compare our product to
compared by
compassionate service
compatibility
compatible
compelled them to buy later
compelling
compelling evidence
compelling force
compelling reason
compelling testimonials
compensate you
compensated with
compensating for
compensation
compensation package
compensation plan
compete with
competitive advantage
competitive advertising

competitive drive
competitive edge
competitive industry
competitive prices
competitor proof
compiled by
complete
complete authority
complete confidentiality
complete honesty
complete information
complete instructions
complete menu
complete package
complete perfection
complete reliability
complete support
complete training
complete truth
completely
completely confidential
completely free
completely free to join
completing a project
completing a task
complex
compliant with
complimentary
compliments your business
compliments your product
composed by
comprehensive index
comprehensive instructions
comprehensive inventory
comprehensive knowledge
comprehensive package
comprehensive solution
compressed
computable

computed by
computer
computer assisted
computer equipment
computer like
computer literate
computer repair
computer training
computerize
computerized
concealed by
concise report
conclusive evidence
conclusive proof
concrete information
concrete solution
condensed version
confession of a
confide in your desires
confidence
confident that you'll
confidential
confidential location
confirm your order
confirmation provided
confirmed by
confusion proof
congratulations
connect the dots
connected
conscious of your
consecutive awards in
consider all alternatives
consider these benefits
consider your
considerate
consistent
consistent accuracy
consistent income

consolidate
consolidated
constant communication
constant interaction with
constant promotional tool
constant revenue stream
constantly improving
constructed by
construction
constructive
constructive advice
constructive approach
consulted by
consulting provided
consumed by
consumer protection
consumer service
contact information
contact us by e-mail
contagious
contemporary
content filled
content rich
contest
continuing relief
continuous
continuous flow of visitors
contract protected
contrary to popular belief
contribute to
contributing
contribution of
control
control your income
control your life style
control your schedule
controversial
convenience
convention like

conventional
conventional size
conversational
conversion cost
conversion ratio
convert every lead
convert into customers
convert more prospects
convert visitors to sales
convert your
convertibility
convertible
convince any skeptic
convince yourself that
convinced that
convincing statistics
cooked by
cool
cooler
coolest
co-op
cooperative
coordinated by
coordinated plan
copy of my bank statement
copyright
coral
core market
corporate
corporate identity
corporate image
corporate secrets
corporation
correct
corruptive proof
cosmetic
cosmic
cost
cost accounting

cost analysis
cost conscious
cost control
cost effective
cost effective advertising
cost efficient
cost of goods sold
cost of living
costly
couldn't live without it
couldn't you
counseled by
countdown to
counted by
counter offensive
counter productive
counteract
counteractive
counterblow
counterclockwise
countered by
counterpart
counting on
countless
country wide
county smart
coupon
courageous
course free
courteous service
courtesy driven
cover virtually every
cover your
cover your butt
coverage provided by
covered by
covering everything
covers a lot of ground
covers all the bases

covers every detail
covers everything
cowboy like
cozy
crackdown on
craft like
crafty
crammed full of
crank
crank out
crank up your promotion
cranks out money
crash and burn
crave your product
crazy
cream of the crop
creamy
create a buying urge
create a lasting impression
create a media frenzy
create a network
create a traffic funnel
create believable ads
create credibility
create impulse spending
create interest
create lifetime customers
create monthly income
create obscene wealth
create profitable deals
create profitable products
create raving fans
create residual income
create your
create your own
create your own products
created by
creating a buzz
creative

creative alternatives
creative invention
credential supported
credentials
credibility
credibility booster
credible
credible guarantee
credible organization
credible story
credit
credit card
credit card processing
credit cards accepted
crime proof
crime ridden
criminal proof
cringe at the thought
crinkled
crisis ready
crisper
crispy
critic proof
critical
critical acclaim
critical acclaimed
critical decision
critical factor
critical issue
critical mass
critical material
critical moment
critical state
critically acclaimed
critically needed
criticism proof
crook proof
cross county
cross merchandising

cross promotion	currently we are offering
cross selling	cursed by
cross the line	curved
crossed by	cushioned
crossover to a new	custom
crowd pleaser	custom built
crowd proof	custom design
crowded by	custom designed
crowned by	custom made
crucial function	customer base
crucial issue	customer care
crucial stage	customer complaints
crucial to own	customer driven
crumbly	customer friendly
crunch the numbers	customer loyalty
crunch time	customer oriented
crunchy	customer oriented company
crush your competition	customer profile
crushed	customer questions
crusty	customer satisfaction
crying free	customer service
crystal clear	customizable
crystal clear sound	customizable links
crystal like	customization
crystallized	customized
cubed	customized affiliate web site
cubic	customized for you
cult like	customized information
cultivated into	customized product
culture	customized version
curable problem	cut and dried
cure your	cut and dry
curiosity driven	cut and dry answers
curled	cut and paste
curly	cut corners
currency converter	cut costs
currency exchange	cut down
current cost	cut out
current price is	cut rate

cut rate price
cut throat
cut to the chase
cut you in on
cut your loses
cutting costs
cutting edge
cyber
cyber ready
cyber space
cybermall
cyberspace
cycle like
cycled
cycloned

Words & Phrases That Start With
"D"

daily
dainty
dairy like
damp
danger
dangerous
dangling hope
dare to be different
dare you to
daring color
daring innovation
dark
darken by
darling
darn
data supported
database chosen
date of
day long
day of
day old
day to day
daydream about
dazzling
dazzling color
dazzling compilation
dazzling event
dead broke
dead deal
dead end
dead on
deadbeat
deadline
deadlocked
deal of the
Dear ( ) Subscriber
Dear (industry) Consultant
Dear (industry) Customer
Dear (item) Dealers

Dear (item) Enthusiast
Dear (item) Seeker
Dear (their name)
Dear Associate
Dear Auction Seller
Dear Bargain Hunter
Dear Bidder
Dear Business Coach
Dear Business Investor
Dear Business Owner
Dear Business Tax Payer
Dear Buyer
Dear CEO
Dear Collector
Dear Copywriter
Dear Customer
Dear Editor
Dear Entrepreneur
Dear Executive
Dear Fellow Business Owner
Dear Friend
Dear Future ( )
Dear Future Millionaire
Dear Home Worker
Dear Home-Based Business Owner
Dear Marketer
Dear Opportunity Seeker
Dear Publisher
Dear Reseller
Dear Sales Representative
Dear Supplier
Dear Surfer
Dear Visitor
Dear Webmaster
Dear Wholesaler
dearly thankful
debated by
debit or credit
debt eliminating

debt free company
debt less
debt ridden budget
debugged
debut
decade long
decaffeinated
decay proof
deceased
deceived by
decent living
decently priced
deceptive competition
decide now
decided by
deciding factor
decipher
decision
decision makers
decision making
decisional
decisive advantage
decisive choice
decisive influence
decisive moment
decode your
deconstructed from
decorated
decreased price
dedicate your
dedicated
dedicated team of
deducted from
deductible
deduction friendly
deed
deep
deep pocket
deep rooted

deepened
deeper
deepest
defeat
defeat your competition
defective until
defend your
defendable
defensible
deferrable
deferred billing
deferred payments
deferred till
defined by
definite answers
definite benefits
definite information
definitely affordable
deflective
defrauding
defrosted
deft free
defused the situation
degree in
delay paying till
delegated by
delete your
deliberate discount
delicacy
delicate
delicious
deliciously
delightful
delightful scent
delightful surprise
delightful taste
delightfully
delighting
deliverable

delivered fast
delivers on their promise
delivery guarantee
delivery mechanism
deluxe
demo
demographically
demonstrate your
demonstrated by
demonstrated skills in
demonstration
demoted to
denied by
denounced by
deodorized
department of
departmental to
dependable
dependable promise
dependably
dependency
dependent upon
deposit
deposited in your bank
depreciated
depreciation
depressed market
depressed over
depth of
descend upon
descent
described with
description
descriptive
design your
designated by
designed by
designed to order
designed to sell

desirable
desired results
desperate deadline
desperate measures
destiny
destroy the competition
destructible
destruction of
destructive
detachable
detail driven
detail oriented
detailed
detailed analysis
detailed description of
detailed instruction
detailed plan
detailed report
detailed research
detailed sales statistics
detailed table of contents
detailed traffic statistics
detailing
detected by
detective
determination
determine the
determine your
determined to help
detrimental to
develop a recognizable brand
develop your
developed by
developed new products
developer tested
developing new
devilish
devoted to
diabolic

diagnosed by
diagonal
diagrammed
dial tone
dial up access
diamond in the rough
diamond like
did you
did you feel
did you know
did you like
did you note that
did you realize
didn't you
die hard customer base
diet proof
dietary
different
difficult economic times
difficult situation
digest version
digital
digital cash
digital delivery
dignified
diligent
dim
dimensional
diminish the
dingy
dinosaur like
dip into
diploma like
diplomatic
dire need
direct
direct access
direct action
direct marketing

direct response
direct selling
directed by
directional
dirt cheap
dirt poor
dirty
dirty secrets
disability friendly
disadvantages of
disaffiliate with
disagree with
disappointed with
disapproval of
disassembles easily
disaster proof
disbelieve the competition
discard your old
disciplined
disclaim any
disclose any
disclosed by
discolored
discontinue using
discount
discount rate
discounted
discover
discover a step by step
discover free
discover how
discover how to
discover new tricks
discover the mistakes that
discover the most important
discover the number one
discover the secrets of
discover what the
discover which

discovered by
discrete packaging
discretion advised
disease proof
disguised by
dish out
dishonest competition
disinfected
dislike your old
dismiss as a
dispatched to
dispensable
dispirited about
display modal
displayed by
displeased with
disposable
disrupt your competition
dissolvable
distinct advantage
distinct trend
distinction between
distinctive competence
distinctly remembered
distinguished
distinguished ability
distorted by
distress about
distributed by
distribution
distribution center
distribution channels
distribution rights
distributor friendly
district runned
disturbed by
ditch your
diverse
diverse background

diverse experience in
diversified
dividable between
divide and conquer
divide your payments
dividends
divine
do I have it right
do it yourself
do something you love
do you ask yourself
do you ever notice that
do you have a problem with
do you know anyone who
do you know what
do you want
do yourself a favor
do...?
doctor approved
doctor recommended
documented
documented facts
dodge the
does...?
doesn't leave anything out
doesn't...?
dollar amount
dollar for dollar
domain friendly
domestic
dominate the
donation of $(no)
don't be fooled by
don't be left out
don't cop out
don't delay
don't even think of ( ) until
don't fall for the hype
don't go away empty handed

don't know how I lived without
don't let (subject) stop you
don't let the chance slip by
don't make another
don't miss out
don't need any employees
don't press you luck
don't take my word for it
dooms day
doorway to
dormant
do's and don'ts
dotcom
double
double barrel
double digit advantage
double digit response rates
double edge
double headed
double header
double hung
double sales
double take
double trouble
double whammy
double your money back
double your revenues
doubled by
doubtful of
down and dirty
down economy
down scale
down the sales path
down to
down to a science
down to earth
down to earth advice
down to the wire
downgraded to

downhill
downline
download a free version of
download it in minutes
download it now
downloadable
downside of not ordering
downsizing
downtrend
dozens of
drafted by
drafty
drag and drop
drama like
dramatic
dramatic breakthrough
dramatic discovery
dramatically increase your sales
draped
drastic mistake
draw the line
drawback
drawing wide interest
drawn out
dream like
dream your
drench in
dressed up
dried
driven
driving force
droopy
drop
drop dead gorgeous
drop down menu
drop shipping
drop the ball
drought stricken
drug free

drum up business
dry
due by
due to popular demand
duplicable
duplicate my success
duplicate our
duplicate your business
duplication proof
durable
duty free
dwarfs other
dyed with
dyer need of
dynamic
dynamite

Words & Phrases That Start With
"E"

each and every
eagerly anticipated
ear piercing
ear splitting
ear steaming
earful of
early bird
early on
early retirement
early stages
earn
earn (no) times your current income
earn an additional $
earn great recognition
earn money
earn money selling
earn money while you sleep
earn more in less time
earn substantial income
earn top dollar
earned income
earned over
earning about
earning potential is enormous
earth shattering
earthbound
earthy materials
ease
ease of distribution
eased up
easier
easiest
easiest way to make money
easily
easily add
easily sell them
easily understood
easy
easy access

easy as pie
easy come, easy go
easy going
easy money
easy payment
easy plan
easy prosperity
easy reference
easy renewal
easy solution
easy to follow
easy to implement
easy to install
easy to read
easy to read and follow
easy to understand
easy to use software
easygoing
eat up your competition
eat your heart out
ebook marketing
ebusiness
ecommerce
economic
economic benefits
economic change
economic climate
economic factors
economic gain
economic growth
economic indicators
economic survival
economical
economy
ecstatic buyers
edge up
edited
educate your audience
educated

educational
effect of
effected by
effective
effective and efficient
effective approach
effective ideas
effective immediately
effective scheme
effectively
efficient
efficient company
efficient service
effort
effort free
effortless
effortless skill
effortlessly
ego less
eight
eighth
either or
ejected from
elaborate
elaborate comfort
elaborate scheme
elaborate style
elapse time
elastic
elastic material
elating
elderly
elected
election held
electric
electricity
electrifying performance
electronic
electronic currency

electronic marketing
electronic publishing
elegance
elegant
elegant shaped
elementary
elevate traffic
elevate your
elevated
elevated level
elevating
eleven
eligibility is limited
eligible for
eliminate all the confusion
eliminate debt
eliminate stress
eliminate work
eliminate your
eliminated
eliminating debt
elite
elude your
elusive
elusiveness
email alert
email marketing
embark on
embarrass by
embedded
embrace our
emerald
emerge as
emergence of
emergency
emerging market
emotion driven
emotional
emotional appeal

emotional response
emotionally charged
empathy
emphasize
empire like
employ our
employable
employed
employee friendly
employer proof
empty
emulate the
enable our
enabled
enchanting
enchanting fragrance
enchanting scene
enchantment
enclosed
encoded with
encounter our
encourage yourself to
encouraged
encrypted
encryption
encyclopedia like
end cold prospecting
end of a
end procrastination
end skepticism
end the daily grind
end user
end your money worries
endangered
endeavor less
endless
endless demand
endless possibilities
endless selection

endless stream of traffic
endless supply
endless supply of ( ) information
endorsed
endorsed by
endorsements
ends today
enduring stability
enduring success
energetic
energize
energize your income
energy friendly
energy saving
enforced
enforced by
engaged
engaged in
engineered
engraved
engraved with
engross yourself
engulfed in
enhance your
enhanced
enhances relationships
enhancing performance
enjoy
enjoy a dream vacation
enjoyable
enjoyable surprise
enjoyed by
enjoyment
enlarge your
enlarged
enlighten by
enlightened
enlightening
enlist our

enlisted
enormous
enormous ability
enormous help
enormous industry
enormous savings
enormous wealth
enraged
enriched
enriching
enroll in
enroll now
ensure yourself
entangle
entangled by
enter here
entering a new
enterprise
enterprising
enterprising entrepreneurs
entertain yourself with
entertained
entertainer like
entertaining
entertainment
enthusiasm
enthusiastic
enthusiastic comments
entice yourself with
enticing
enticing choice
enticing incentive
enticing offer
entire price of
entirely up to you
entrancing
entrepreneur
entrust
entry level

envious of
environment
environmental
environmental concerns
environmentally friendly
environmentally safe
environmentally sound
envision having
envy
epic adventure
epic proportions
epidemic like
equal
equal terms
equipment
equipped with
equity
era of
erasable
erased from
erotic
erotica
errand free
error proof
errorless
erupt your
erupt your cash
escape proof
escape your
escaping the daily grind
escorted by
essence of
essential
essential component
essential goods
essential ingredients
essential knowledge
essential nutrients
establish

establish rapport
establish yourself as
established
established classic
established tradition
estimated
eternal problem
eternity
ethical
ethical procedures
ethically increase your profits
ethics
evaluated by
evaporated
even
even for busy people
even terms
event of
eventually you
ever lasting
ever present
ever wonder how
everlasting comfort
everlasting profits
every (no)th customer will
every entrepreneur
every little bit helps
every minute counts
every wonder
everyone experiences
everyone is joining
everyone is talking about
everything exposed
everything from ( ) to ( )
everything still in tact
everything you always wanted to
know about
everything you may have heard
about

everything you need
everything you need to know
evidence from
exact
exact instructions
exact timetable
exactly
exactly how
exactly how to
exactly what
exactly what I've been looking
exactly what you get
examination less
examined by
example
examples of how
exceed your goals
exceeding expectations
excellence
excellent
excellent authority
excellent craftsmanship
excellent credentials
excellent credit
excellent payment structure
excellent quaity
excellent quality
excellent skills
except our
exceptional ability
exceptional antique
exceptional condition
exceptional facility
exceptional honesty
exceptional qualifications
exceptional quality
exceptional service
exceptionally high incomes
exceptionally reliable

excess of
excessively
exchange it for
exciting
exciting adventure
exciting challenge
exciting destination
exciting developments
exciting discovery
exciting invention
exciting news
exciting results
exciting revelation
exclude the $(no)
exclusive
exclusive access
exclusive information
exclusive news
exclusive privilege
exclusive product
exclusive rights
exclusivity
excuse me but
execute our
executed
executive
executive like
executive strength
executive summary
exempt by
exempted
exemption
exercise free
exercised by
exhausted from
exhibited at
exhilarated by
exhilarating adventure
exhilarating news

existing customers
exotic location
exotic taste
expand
expand your marketers
expandability
expandable
expanded
expanding income
expands your knowledge
expansion driven
expect a lot
expedited by many
expendable income
expenditures
expense
expensive experimentation
expensive looking
experience happiness
experience included
experience the
experienced
experienced as
experienced in all aspects of
experienced in all facets of
experienced in all phases of
experiential
experiment like
experimented
expert
expert choice
expert in your field
expert only information
expert opinion
expert solutions
expert testimonials
expertise
experts agree
experts won't share this

explained by

explanation

explicit

explode

explode your orders

exploded

exploit

explore new opportunities

explore your

explosion in profits

explosive

explosive growth

explosive influence tactics

exported

exposed

exposure

express

express ordering

expressed

expressible

exquisite color

exquisite elegance

exquisite pleasure

exquisitely detailed

extend your

extended

extensible

extensive experience

extensive involvement

extensive marketing

extensive training

exterminate

external

extinct

extinction proof

extinguished by many as

extra

extra energy

extra exposure

extra incentives

extra insurance

extra money

extra source of income

extracted from

extraction proof

extraordinary collection

extraordinary resemblance

extraordinary success

extrasensory

extravagant

extravagant gift

extreme

extreme accuracy

extreme caution

extreme persuasion strategies

extremely hard to find

extremely versatile

eye candy

eye catching

eye catching style

eye opening

eye opening advice

eye pleaser

eye popping

eye startling

eyebrow raising

eyewitness accounts

eyewitnesses

ezine advertising

ezine friendly

Words & Phrases That Start With
"F"

fabricated proof	fame
fabulous	fame and fortune
fabulous adventure	familiar
fabulous collection	familiarized by
fabulous taste	family
face up	family run
face up to reality	famine proof
face value	famous
faceless	fan driven
fact	fancy
fact finding	fancy schmancy
fact sheet	fantasies
factor in	fantasize learning
factoring	far and wide
factory like	far fetched
facts and figures	far flung
factual	far more than I expected
factual material	far out
fad like	far reaching consequences
fad proof	far seeing
fail proof	far surpasses anything
fail safe	fascinating figures
fail safe system	fascinating ideas
fail safe tests	fascinating information
failure	fascinating results
faint hit of	fashion
fair	fashion conscious
fair and square	fashion friendly
fair market value	fashionable mix
fair methods	fashioned
fair price	fast
fair shake	fast and easy access
fair value	fast and furious
faith	fast break
faithfully	fast breaking news
fake out	fast delivery
fall back on	fast distribution
fall in love with	fast food
fallen to $(no)	fast growing

fast growing collection
fast growing market
fast moving
fast pace
fast results
fast rising
fast service
faster
fastest
fat free
fatal
fate
father from the truth
favorable image
favorite
fear of
feared by
fearless
feasible ideas
feast on
feast or famine
featured
features
federal
fee less
feed yourself
feedback friendly
feel like a million
felt by many
festival like
festive
few and far between
few clicks of the mouse
few disagree
few employees
fewer the better
fiber like
fictional
field of

fielded by
figure driven
figure pointing
figured by
fill in
fill in the blank
filled with
filler
fills the bill
filmed at
filter proof
filthy rich
final offer
finalized today
finance
financed
financial
financial abundance
financial advice
financial advisor
financial collapse
financial crisis
financial dreams
financial freedom
financial gain
financial goal
financial independence
financial position
financial security
financial statement
financially beneficial
financially independent life
find extra cash
find hidden profits
find out a easier way
find out how to
find smarter ways
find success
finders fee

fine
fine accent
fine and dandy
fine antique
fine craftsmanship
fine grained
fine quality
fine reputation
fine texture
fine tune your
fine tune your biz
fine workmanship
finely crafted
finish by
fire breathing
fire like
fire off
fire proof
fire your boss
fired up
fireproof materials
firm
firm action
firm believer in
firm commitment
firm hold
firm policy
firm support
firmly placed
first
first and foremost
first class
first class company
first come first served
first degree
first generation
first hand
first hand experience
first hand facts

first hand report
first line of defense
first of its kind
first place
first priority
first prize
first rate
first round
first strike
firsthand experience
fist punching
fist squeezing
fit
fit for a king
fits all
fits in your pocket
fits your budget
five
five star
five star rating
fix up
fixable
flabbergasted
flame proof
flannel
flaring
flash by
flat
flat fee
flaunt it
flavor less
flawless
flawless integrity
flawless system
flee from
flex your
flexible
flimsy
flip over

flirt with
flood of
flood of money
flood of visitors
floodgates of success
floored by
floral
flourishing business
flowing
fluent in
fluffy
fluid like
fluke
flurry of
flush out
fly by night
focus on
focused
foldable
follow though
follow up
follow up message
follow your dreams
follow your heart
follow your instincts
follow your passions
followed through
follows directions
follows through
foolish
foolproof
foolproof ideas
foolproof methods
foot loose
foot stumping
for a beginner or pro
for a novice or expert
for a number of years
for a select few

for beginners or veterans
for better or for worse
for example
for less than $ you can
for less than the cost of
for most any budget
for serious collectors only
for the hell of it
for the low price of $
for the month of
for the next (no) buyers we
for those of you planning
forbidden
forbidden luxury
forbidden secrets
force field of
forced by
forced matrix
forecasted by
foreclose on
forefront of
foreign
foremost expert on
forensic like
foreplay
foresight in
foretell the future
forever
forfeit your
forgery proof
forget about
forgetful
forgivable
forgive us for
form and substance
formalized offer
formatted with
formed by
former customer

formidable challenges
formula
formula for success
formulated with
forthcoming
fortunate
fortune
forum of
fossil like
foul
foul smelling
found out
foundation
founded by
founders of
four
four star
four wheeled
fourth
foxy
fraction of
fragile
fragile economy
fragrance
fragrance free
framed
framework
franchised
franchising
fraud proof
freak of
freak out
freaky
free
free advertising
free and clear
free articles
free bonus
free booklet

free classified ad
free consulting
free distribution rights
free ebook
free ecourse
free email consolidation
free email support
free enterprise
free excerpt
free exposure
free ezine
free ezine submission
free flowing
free gift
free gift subscription
free Internet access
free lesson
free market
free newsletter
free parts
free personal help
free publicity
free report
free reprint rights
free resell rights
free ride
free sample
free samples or trials
free seminar
free service
free shipping
free software
free standing
free subscription
free support
free telephone consulting
free to join
free training
free trial

free trial download
free up your time
free vacation certificate
free web site
free your schedule
freebie
freedom
freelanced
freelancing as
freely
freeze dry
freeze proof
freeze up
frenzy
frequency
frequent
fresh
fresh and targeted
fresh detail
fresh information
fresh insights
fresh look
fresh originality
fresh perspective
fresh scent
fresh thinking
fresher
freshly made
friction proof
fried
friend like
friendly
friendly advice
friendly terms
frighten by
frigid
fringe benefits
frisky
from rags to riches

from start to finish
from the bottom up
front line
fronted by
frost like
frosted
frown upon
frozen
frugal
frugal times
fruity
fuel efficient
fuel to the fire
fugitive like
fulfill
fulfilled
fulfilling a dream
fulfilling a fantasy
fulfillment driven
full
full blooded
full blossom
full blown
full bodied
full bodied taste
full circle
full course
full coverage
full faced
full fledged
full grown
full hearted
full independence
full length
full level intelligence
full page ad
full scale
full service
full size book

full solution
full term
full throttle
full time
fully
fully assembled
fully automated
fully documented
fully insured
fully prepared
fully restored
fully searchable
fully trackable
fun
function less
functional
fund raiser
fundamental
fundamental business principles
fundamental component
fundamental goals
funded by
fungus proof
funky
funnel
funnel in business
funny
furious with
furnished
future
future earnings
future of

Words & Phrases That Start With "G"

gadget

gag gift

gain

gain an edge

gain an enormous following

gain authority

gain control of your life

gain instant

gain instant recognition

gain new leads and customers

gain pleasure

gain prestigious

gain status

gain the upper hand

gain valuable experience

gaining a promotion

gaining a skill

gaining a talent

gaining an advantage

gaining free publicity

gaining freedom

gaining knowledge

gaining popularity

gaining time

galactic

galaxy like

gallery of

gamble less

gambling

game like

game plan

gamesmanship

gang up

gangster like

garbage proof

garnish with

gas generated

gas less

gas powered

gated

gateway to

gathered by

gauge your

gear down

gear less

gear shifting

gear up

geared for

gel

gelled together

gem like

gems

gender friendly

gender specific

general

generate a huge response

generate cash on demand

generate consistent revenue

generate instant cash

generate leads

generate more leads

generate qualified targeted leads

generate sales

generated

generic

generosity

generous hospitality

generous offer

generous portion

generous terms

genetic

genius

gentle

gently

genuine

genuine commitment

genuine improvement

genuine offer

genuine opportunity
genuine satisfaction
geographical
germ free
germ less
get $ worth of bonus gifts
get (no) free gifts
get (no) page views
get (no) surprise bonuses
get (no)% off of selling price
get a (no)% discount
get a bang out of
get a free subscription to
get a high ranking
get a load off
get a maximum return
get a piece of the pie
get a sneak peak at some
get across
get all dolled up
get an edge
get around
get away
get back on your feet
get direct access to
get dozens of
get every technique I use
get every tool I use
get everything you need to
get expert advice on
get free advertising
get in
get into the swing of things
get it without delay
get more traffic
get on auto pilot
get on the stick
get one under your belt
get out of debt

get paid
get paid forever
get readers interested
get reciprocal links
get repeat visitors
get results
get rich quick
get rid of financial frustration
get rid of money problems
get spectacular results
get started immediately
get started in minutes
get started overnight
get started today
get the ball rolling
get the buzz
get the facts
get the final word
get the freedom you want
get the goods on
get the inside track
get the last laugh
get the most for your money
get the picture
get the upper hand
get them to buy
get these incentives
get to the top
get together
get top placement
get top rankings
get up the nerve
get with it
get your feet wet
get your foot in the door
get your hands on
get your prospect's attention
getting a bargain
getting a discount

getting a raise
getting intense interest
getting over obstacles
ghost like
ghostly
giant
giant like
gift
gift certificate
gifted
gifted marketer
gigantic industry
gigantic profit
gimmick proof
give and take
give away
give back
give in
give me a chance
give up
give you an insiders
giveaway rights
giveaways
gives you more flexibility
gives you new insight
glad
gladly
glamorized
glamour driven
glare less
glaring
glass
glass clear
glassy
glazed
glimmer of
glimmer of hope
glimmering
glitch proof

glittering
global
global achiever
global commerce
global market
global marketing
globalize
globe like
gloomy
glorified by
glorious
glory
gloss
glossy
glowing
glowing acknowledgments
glowing forecast
glowing reviews
glowing testimonials
glued together
go
go along for the ride
go down in history
go for broke
go for it
go for the gold
go the distance
go to town
goal
goal oriented
goal setting
goes both ways
going away from
going bananas over
going like clockwork
going on
going public
going through the roof
going value

gold
gold digger
gold medal
gold mine at your fingertips
gold mine of secrets
gold plated
gold rush
golden
golden opportunity
gone instantly
good
good advice
good afternoon
good and ready
good as gold
good by
good customer service
good day
good deal
good evening
good faith
good health
good humored
good investment
good judgment
good listener
good looking
good luck
good night
good quality
good reviews
good sense
good year
goods
goodwill
goof proof
goofy
gossip
governed

government
government established
governmental
grab their attention
grab your
grab your share
grace period
graceful
graceful acknowledgments
grade a
gradual adjustment
gradual increase
graduate
graduated from
grainy
grand
grand adventure
grand opening
grand prize
grand scale
grand slam
grand times
grand tour
grant yourself
granted by
grape flavored
graphic
grass roots
grassy
grateful
gratification
gratifying
grave consequences
gray colored
greasy
great
great bargain
great deal
great deal of money

great for beginners
great for novices
great significance
great wealth
greater
greatest
greed
greedy
green colored
grenade like
grief stricken
grim results
gritty
gross
gross earnings
gross income
gross revenue
gross sales
ground breaking
ground breaking findings
ground breaking solutions
ground floor
ground floor opportunity
ground out
ground shaking
ground speed
grounded
group like
group ware
grouped
grow
grow up
grow your business
grow your practice
growing
growing commitment
growing competition
growing craze
growing day by day

growing demand
growth fund
growth industry
growth patterns
growth potential
growth segment
grueling hours
guarantee
guarantee your success
guaranteed
guaranteed income
guaranteed success
guaranteed to work
guaranteed visitors
guarantees
guard against
guarded
guarded secrets
guardian angel
guess
guesswork
guest
guide
guided
guided tour
guiding force
guilt
guilty
gunning
guru
gut like
gutsy
gutter less

Words & Phrases That Start With "H"

habit	handsome benefit
habit buying	handsome offer
habit forming	handsome profit
habitual	handy
hacker proof	handy guide
haggle the price	handy order form
hair raising	handy reference
hairy	hang onto your hat
half baked	happy
half hearted	happy alternative
half off	happy feeling
half price	hard bitten
halftone	hard core
hand blistering	hard drive
hand blown	hard earned
hand carved	hard earned dollars
hand crafted	hard earned money
hand held	hard facts
hand made	hard hearted
hand painted	hard hitting
hand picked	hard hitting appeal
hand powered	hard liner
hand set	hard nose
hand stamped	hard nosed approach
hand stenciled	hard offer
hand woven	hard one
hand written	hard pressed
handier	hard shelled
handle the volume	hard to beat
handling	hard to find
hands free	hard to get
hands free income	hard to pin down
hands free system	hard to resist
hands on	hard up
hands on demonstration	hard wired
hands on experience	hard working people
hands on information	hard, cold facts
hands on training	hardball
handsome	hardship

hardware
hardworking
harmful
harmless
harness
harness the power
harsh economic times
harshly
harvest
has been
hassle free
haunted by
haunting beauty
have a ball
have a heart
have access within minutes
have it made
have money to burn
have the time of your life
have them in your pocket
have you
have you been trying to
have you ever asked yourself
have you ever purchased an
have you ever wanted
have you ever wished
haven't seen it anywhere else
haven't you
having a fulfilling career
having authority
having excellent credit
having high investment returns
having things easier
having things faster
hazardous free
head fast
head over heels
head spinning
head start

head to head
head turner
head turning
headache proof
headline
heads up
headway
healing
healthy
healthy flow of customers
healthy income
healthy portion
heard working
heart felt
heart pounding
heart rendering
heart stirring discovery
heart to heart advice
heartfelt
heartfelt appeal
hearty
hearty nutrients
heat proof
heat up
heat up your sales
heated
heaven
heaven sent
heaven sent opportunity
heavenly
heavier
heavily armed
heavy
heavy duty
heavy handed
heavy hitter
heavy weight
hefty
hefty gain

hefty profits
heighten
hell bent
hell like
hell or high water
hello
help
help desk
help you personally
helped many
helpful
helpful invention
helpful reference
helpful service
helpless
helps you
helps you ( ) every step of the way
here are my credentials
here is a summary
here is how you can
here to stay
here's (no) reasons why you
here's a fact for you
here's a list of common
here's a quick recap
here's a small sample
here's a summary of
here's my actual check (your affiliate check)
here's my web site stats
here's proof
here's something that will
here's the bottom line
here's what other say (testimonials)
here's what you'll learn
here's what you'll receive
here's your opportunity to
hero like
heroic

heroic status
hesitant with
hi
hidden
hidden gold mine
hidden secrets
hidden strengths
hidden wealth
high
high achievement
high and mighty
high budget
high caliber
high click through rate
high conversion ratio
high cut
high definition
high degree of
high demand
high end features
high energy level
high ethical standards
high expectations
high flying
high frequency
high grade
high hopes
high impact strategies
high income products
high intensity
high key agenda
high level
high level of expertise
high level strategies
high margin products
high octane
high paying
high payoff
high percentage

high performance
high pitched
high potential
high powered
high pressure
high priced
high priority
high probability
high productive output
high profile
high profile industries
high profit margin
high profit potential
high quality
high quality company
high quality goods
high quality products
high ranking
high results
high return
high return investment
high rise
high rise enterprise
high risk
high roller
high security
high speed
high speed traffic
high spirited
high standards
high status lifestyle
high strung
high tech
high tech innovation
high tech service
high tension
high ticket items
high turnover
high velocity

high voltage
high wage
higher
higher click rates
higher conversions
higher income
higher paying
higher profit margins
higher sales conversion
highest
highest paid people
highest paying clients
highest quality
highest recommendation ever
highest recommendations
highest response anywhere
highest standards
highlighted
highly acclaimed seminar
highly ambitious
highly articulate
highly competitive
highly complexed
highly customizable
highly endorsed
highly guarded
highly motivated
highly organized
highly persuasive
highly prosperous people
highly rated ( )
highly regarded
highly respected
highly selective
highly sensitive information
highly skilled
highly skilled marketers
highly sophisticated
highly specialized

highly trained	hopeful situation
hilarious	hordes of customers
hire us	hordes of visitors
hired by	horizon expanding
historic	horizontal
historic treasure	horrendous figures
historical	horrible conditions
historical material	horribly
history making	horrified by
history of prior successes	hospitable
history rich	hospitality driven
hit and miss	hosted by
hit counter spinning	hostile competition
hit or miss	hostile takeover
hit the bull's eye	hot
hit the jackpot	hot and cold
hit their sweet spots	hot business model
hit's the spot	hot commodity
hold prospects attention	hot issue
holiday	hot product
holiday favorite	hot selling
hollow	hot tempered
hollowed out	hot ticket
home based business	hotheaded
home business	hotshot
home grown	hotter
home made	hottest
home office	hour long
home stead	hourly
homemade	how a simple
honest	how and where to
honest methods	how and why to
honest truth	how anyone can
honesty	how come
honor	how do you
honorable	how does
honorary	how I ( ) in one week
hook, line and sinker	how I get at least
hope	how I made $

how I once	how to identify
how I took a	how to increase
how important is	how to install
how I've earned	how to instantly
how many times have you	how to know exactly
how often to	how to know if
how one man	how to launch a
how one person	how to legally
how one woman	how to literally
how to	how to locate
how to absolutely	how to maintain
how to actually see	how to make
how to add	how to manage
how to always	how to never again
how to automatically	how to obtain
how to avoid	how to operate
how to become an	how to overcome
how to build	how to pick
how to buy	how to present
how to choose	how to produce
how to come up with	how to promote
how to create	how to pull in $
how to decide	how to quickly
how to design	how to reduce
how to determine your	how to roll out
how to develop	how to select
how to double	how to sell
how to earn	how to send
how to eliminate	how to set up
how to ensure	how to spend
how to establish	how to spot
how to find	how to start
how to gain	how to stop
how to generate	how to take
how to get	how to tap into
how to get rid of	how to tell if
how to get your hands on	how to triple
how to give your	how to turn
how to have	how to use

how understanding the
how would you feel knowing
how would you like to
how you can
how...?
howdy
huge amount
huge collection
huge compilation
huge discount
huge fortune
huge industry
huge money maker
huge proportions
huge quantities
huge selection
huge success
human like
humane
humble
humbling display
humorless
humorous
hundreds
hungry
hungry crowd of customers
hunky dory
hurry
hustle and bustle
hustle proof
hygiene
hyped up
hyper feeling
hyperactive
hypnotic
hypnotic effects
hypnotize
hypnotized prospects
hypoallergenic

Words & Phrases That Start With
"I"

I (benefit) (no) thousand in (no) weeks
I (benefit) in (no) days
I (benefit) in (no) weeks
I (benefit) over (no) %
I (benefit) up to (no) %
I (benefit)(no) pounds in (no) months
I (benefits) leas than (no) hours
I almost bought it again
I am about to tell you a
I am excited to
I appreciate your interest
I couldn't wait to
I don't care if you're
I don't care what
I don't have to convince you of
I don't want to waste
I first got involved in
I graduated from college
I grew up in (location) in the (year)
I have a confession to make
I have a degree in
I have first hand experience
I heard from
I heard on (source) that
I highly recommend
I just have to say
I know from experience
I know this sounds
I know you
I know you don't have
I know your busy
I know your skeptical
I know you've been
I love it
I normally charge
I normally charge up to $
I picture you

I promise to
I rarely endorse products but
I rate it (no) out of (no)
I read in a (source) that
I remember back about ( ) years
I saw on (source) that
I sense you
I stand behind the product
I think you'll agree
I trust you'll
I was blown away
I was reluctant at first
I was skeptical but
I would have paid
icon like
I'd like to make you a promise
idea driven
idea generation
ideal
ideal choice
ideal condition
ideal customer
ideas
identical
identifiable
identification checked
identified
idiot proof
idiotic
idol
idolized by
if I can do it you can
if I were you
if you
if you already
if you are looking for a simple
if you are seriously
if you aren't familiar with
if you buy now

if you could have
if you give me (no) minutes to
if you learn nothing else
if you like the idea of
if you really want to
if you thought
if you want a
if you want the answers to
if you want to know how
if you would like to
if you would like to learn
if you're currently
if you're like me
if you're like most
if you're looking for
if you're planning to
if you're ready to
if you're serious about
if you're tired of
if you've been looking
if you've been wanting to
if you've ever thought about
if you've ever wondered
if you've read every
if you've tried to
if you've watched
ignitable
ignite your
ignite your profits
ignite your sales
ignorant proof
ignore the
ill advised
I'll also throw in
I'll assume you've
I'll be completely honest with you about
I'll bet you anything that
ill feeling

I'll get straight to the point
I'll help you
ill judged
I'll keep my word
I'll make you a promise
ill mannered
ill nature
I'll personally guarantee
I'll refund your money
I'll refund your purchase
I'll show you how to
I'll show you the following
I'll show you where
I'll teach you
I'll tell you exactly how to
I'll throw in (no) bonuses
illegal
illuminated
I'm about to reveal to you
I'm absolutely amazed
I'm confident that
I'm definitely impressed
I'm going to show you
I'm no rookie
I'm not going to waste your time
I'm not kidding
I'm sensing that you
I'm so (emotion) today
I'm speechless
I'm sure you agree with
I'm sure you heard of
I'm sure you know from experience
I'm sure you'll agree that
I'm sure you're
I'm very satisfied
image driven
imaginable
imaginary
imagination friendly

imagine making $
imagine that
imagined by
immeasurable
immeasurable importance
immediate
immediate access
immediate action
immediate cash flow
immediate cash surge
immediate change
immediately
immediately after you order
immediately downloadable
immense appeal
immense fortune
immense improvement
immense relief
immense satisfaction
immense size
immerse yourself with
immobilize your
immoral
immortal
immovable
immune to
impacted by
impeccable
impeccable guide
impeccable policy
impeccable reputation
imperial
implemented
important
important addition
important factor
imported
impose your
impossible

impossible to fail
impractical
impress your
impression driven
impressive
impressive ability
impressive demonstration
impressive findings
impressive packaging
impressive statistics
impressive technology
imprinted
improper to
improve
improve customer retention
improve customer service
improve every area of your life
improve link popularity
improve your business
improve your lifestyle
improve your sales
improved
improvement
improvise
impulse buying
impulse like
impulsive
in
in (month/year)
in (no) or less
in (year)
in (year) I
in a big way
in a few minutes
in a flash
in business for (no.) decades
in case
in charge of
in close

in constant demand
in demand
in demand product
in depth
in depth analysis
in depth report
in depth study
in excellent condition
in flesh and blood
in full swing
in hot pursuit
in house
in less than no time
in line
in minutes
in my humble opinion
in my opinion
in order to ( ) you need
in prelaunch
in record numbers
in season
in seconds
in short supply
in stock
in store
in style
in the bag
in the black
in the lap of luxury
in the long run
in the next (no) minutes
in the nick of time
in the red
in this article you're going to
in this day and age
in this letter you're going to
in this report you're going to
in today's
in your best interests

in your spare time
inactive
inappropriate
in-between jobs
inbound
incalculable profits
incalculable worth
incapable of
incentives
inch by inch
incidental
included with
includes (no) issues
includes a high tech formula for
includes useful resources
income
income enhancing
income literally overnight
income on the line
income statement
income stream
income tax
incoming
incomparable
incompatible of
incomplete
inconceivable
inconclusive
inconsiderate businesses
inconspicuous
incontestable
incontestable proof
inconvenient
incorporate
incorporated
incorporation
incorrect numbers
increase
increase affiliate commissions

increase leads
increase leverage
increase perceived value
increase profits
increase readership
increase renewals
increase sales
increase sales anytime
increase subscribers
increase the dollar value
increase their average order amount
increase your
increase your bank account
increase your cash flow
increase your closing ratio
increase your popularity
increase your sales volume
increase your success
increased
increasing
increasing affiliate partners
increasing profits
increasing sales
increasing traffic
incredible
incredible announcement
incredible results
incredible sight
incredible sums of money
incredibly easy
incredibly low budget
indebted to helping you
indeed you can
indefinite supply
independence
independent
independent company
independent contractor
independent professionals

indestructible
indestructible material
indexed by
indispensable
indispensable component
indisputable evidence
indisputable proof
individual effort
indoor
indulge in
industrial
industrial strength
industrialized
industry
industry experts
industry leader
industry leading
industry secrets
industry's leading experts
ineffective
inefficient
ineligible for
inestimable benefits
inexpensive
infamous
inferior to
infiltrate your
infinite benefits
infinite possibilities
infinity
inflatable
inflated prices
inflation prone economy
inflation proof
influence
influence buying behavior
influence others
influence your prospects
influenced by

infomercial
inform yourself on
informal
information
information highway
information superhighway
informational
informed
informed advice
ingenious
ingenious design
ingenious mechanics
ingenious methods
ingenious tactics
ingenious technique
ingredient
inhabited by
inherit our
inhuman
inhumane
initial
initial public offering
initially employed
injury free
inner
inner circle
innermost
innocent
innovated
innovation
innovative
innovative approach
innovative concept
innovative creation
innovative skills
innovator in
inopportune time
ins and outs
insane

insane amounts of traffic
insane not to buy
insanely profitable
inscribed with
insecure
inside
inside knowledge
insider discoveries
insider information
insider knowledge
insider secrets to
insightful
inspected by
inspection checked
inspiration
inspired
installation free
installed
installed by
installment plan
instant
instant access
instant access product
instant acclaim
instant e-mail notifications
instant fortune
instant impacted
instant magic
instant message
instant money machine
instant reference
instant relief
instant results
instant success
instantaneous
instantly
instantly learn
instituted by
institution like

instructed
instructional
instructions
instrumental in
insubstantial amount of
insufficient
insufficient income
insulated
insurable
insurance
insure yourself
insured by
intacted
intangible
integral part
integrate your
integrated by
integrity
intellect
intellectual
intellectual atmosphere
intellectual property
intellectually
intellectually appealing
intelligence
intelligent
intense
intense commitment
intensify your sales
intensive study
intent on
interactive
interactive experience
interchangeable
interest free
interest free findings
interest less
interest rate
interesting

interesting adventure
interesting developments
interesting invention
interfaced with
interior designed
interlocking
intermediate
internal problem
internally secret
international
international acclaim
international attention
international best seller
international reputation
internationally known
Internet
Internet access
Internet marketing
Internet marketing guru
Internet presence
interpreted by
interrupt your
intervention
interview free
interviewed by
intimate moment
intoxicating
intriguing
intriguing collection
intriguing details
intriguing features
intriguing ideas
intriguing results
intriguing scene
introducing
introduction
introductory offer
introductory price
introductory price of only

intruder proof
intuition driven
intuitive
invalid
invaluable
invaluable advice
invaluable facts
invaluable help
invent your future
invented
invention
inventive
inventive tactics
inventory controlled
inverted
invest in our product today
invest now
invest today and receive
invested in
investigate
investigated by
investigation
investigative
investing
investment
investment bank
investment banker
investment quality
investor like
invincible
invisible
invite your friends
invited by
inviting
inviting offer
invoiced by
involuntary
involve yourself
involved in

iron like
ironclad
irrefutable
irreplaceable
irresistible
irresistible appeal
irresistible magnetism
irresistible sales letter
irresistible temptation
irresponsibility
is ( ) a problem for you
is it possible that
isolate yourself from
issued by
it actually delivers
it blows my mind
it can't be matched
it can't hurt
it could mean the difference
it could take you years
it doesn't matter how
it far exceeded my wildest
it has been about (no) years since
it is by far
it is for people that
it over delivers
it seems that everywhere
it simply works
it surprises me how most people
it took (time) of research
it walks you through
it was just another typical day
it would take several
it's (time) on a (day)
it's a fact that
it's a steal
it's absolutely crucial you learn
it's all covered in
it's all here

it's allowed me to
it's almost ( ) years old
it's better than nothing
it's common knowledge that
it's critical to have this information
it's important to understand that
it's in our (no) year
it's just what you need
it's more like a library
it's not for everyone
it's not the same old ( ) you use to
it's numbered
it's quite obvious
it's sold over (no) copies
it's that good
it's the only ( ) that
itty bitty
I've discovered a
I've found the secret to
I've just put together
I've personally found
I've recently
I've recently developed a
I've sold over $
I've taught
I've taught ( ) seminars about
I've written
I've written over ( ) on

Words & Phrases That Start With
"J"

jacked up fees
jam packed
jargon free
jargon less
jaw dropping
jazz up your sales
jealous feeling
jealously guarded
jeopardizing your
jerked around
jet lagged
jewel like
job satisfaction
jobless
join now
join our affiliate program
join our reseller program
join the (no)% who
join the club
join today
joined by
joint enterprise
joint facility
joint venture
joint venture opportunities
joyful
judged by
judgment
judgmental
judicial like
juicy
juicy profit
juicy story
jump on the bandwagon
jump start your
jump start your orders
junky looking
just $ for a membership
just a few minutes

just a taste of the
just between you and me
just cash the checks
just cause
just last week
just one (benefit) will pay for
just plug in and sell
just published
just released
just sit back and relax
just small sample of
just the other day
just the ticket
just what the doctor ordered
justice driven
justifiable alternative
justified price

Words & Phrases That Start With
"K"

keen delight
keen insights
keep (no)% of the profits
keep 100% of each sale
keep customers
keep customers happy
keep every penny
keep prospects interested
keep quiet about
keep the free bonuses
keep the profits rolling
keep their eyeballs locked
keep them glued to your
keep then on the edge of their seat
keep this to yourself
keep up with the competition
keep up with the times
keep your costs down
keep your customers
keeps you abreast of
keeps you ahead of the game
keeps you informed with
key account
key fact
key issue
keynote
kick butt
kick off
kick start your business
kid friendly
kill two birds with on stone
killer
killer marketing schemes
killer reviews
killer ways
kind act
kindhearted
king like
kiss your boss goodbye

kissable
knee deep
knee jerking
knee slapping
knock on wood
knock out
know how
know how to
know the ropes
knowledge
knowledge about
knowledge base
knowledge incentive
knowledge of
knowledge sources
knowledgeable
knowledgeable service
known by

Words & Phrases That Start With
"L"

lab tested
labor less
labor saving equipment
laboring
laced
lackluster
ladylike
laid back
laid off
lame
land locked
landmark
landmark announcement
large
large amount
large collection
large company
large earning potential
large market
large minded
large package
large savings
large scale
large share
large size
larger
larger than life
largest
largest ever
lasering
laser like precision
last
last but not least
last chance
last gasp
last minute
last resort
last stand
last straw

last week
last year
lasting
lasting impact
lasting impression
lasting legend
lasting reputation
lasting solution
lasting stability
lasting success
latch on to
late notice
latest
latest craze
latest fad
latest sensation
latest technology
launched today
lavish
lavish amount
lavish gift
lavish praise
law abiding
law like
lawful
lay it on the line
lay your cards on the table
layaway
lazy
lazy mans
lead generation
lead in
lead yourself to
leadership
leadership qualities
leading
leading case
leading cause
leading edge

leading indicator
leading motive
leading question
leak proof
lean
leaner
leaps and bounds
learn
learn about all the
learn closely guarded
learn everyday
learn everything from a to z
learn everything from start to finish
learn everything I've learn
learn exactly what
learn fresh tips
learn from my experience
learn from my mistakes
learn from other pros
learn how to
learn little known resources
learn new
learn to
learn to harness
learn to write
lease or buy
least expensive
least known
leather like
leave the rat race
leaves no stone unturned
lectured by
led by
left handed
leg kicking
leg pulling
leg up
legacy
legal

legal advice
legal jointure
legalized
legally
legally and ethically
legally increase your sales
legally steal business
legend
legendary
legendary discovery
legendary masterpiece
legendary success
legendary supreme
legendary tycoon
legislation proof
legit
legitimacy
legitimate
legitimate concerned
legitimate opportunity
legitimate source of cash
leisure like
leisurely
lengthy study
lessons learned
let down
let me introduce myself
let me share with you
let me tell you the story
let your hair down
lethal
lethal mistakes
let's examine the
let's get down to business
let's have it
let's talk about
level of service
level off
leveled

levels of performance
leveraging the media
liability
liberty
license to resell
licensed rights
licensing
licensing agreement
life and death
life changing
life changing secrets
life giving
life less
life like
life of riches
life or death
life saving
life threatening
lifeblood
lifesaver
lifestyle you deserve
lifetime
lifetime commission
lifetime commitment
lifetime guarantee
lifetime membership
lifetime of wealth
lifetime revenue
lifetime traffic
light
light minded
light up your traffic
light weight
light years ahead of competition
lightened
lightening fast results
lightest
lightly scented
lightweight

likable
like a million
like a ton of bricks
like clockwork
like gangbusters
like minded
like new
like you, I have
limber
limit buying resistance
limit your
limited
limited access
limited availability
limited budget
limited edition
limited no. of affiliates
limited time
limitless
line of action
line of communication
line of credit
line of duty
line of products
links to
lip puckering
lip smacking
liquidated
little
little by little you
little effort
little known
little known techniques
little money
little time
little used
live
live dangerously
live now

live smarter not harder
live very comfortably
live your dream
livelihood
lively
livid color
living legend
living proof
loaded
loaded with
loan you
loaves of
lobbied by
local
localized
locally sold
locatable
located in
lock and key
lock out
lock, stock and barrel
locked
log in
log on
logic driven
logical
logical addition
logical choice
lonely
long
long abandon
long awaited
long distance
long established
long established industry
long haul
long lasting
long lasting influence
long lasting partnerships

long lasting relief
long legged
long lived
long lost edition
long over due
long range
long range strategy
long range threat
long standing
long standing commitment
long standing policy
long standing relationship
long standing tradition
long suffering
long term
long term business success
long term commitment
long term compensation
long term gain
long term hospitality
long term remedy
long term residual traffic
long tern vision
long winded
longevity
look at our client list
look at these case studies
look at these comments
look at what's inside
look like a million dollars
look out
look up our
look what's included
looks so real
loose
loose cannon
loose fit
lose your
lost cause

lost opportunity
lots of cash
lottery like
loud
loud and clear
lovable
love
love at first sight
love it or leave it
loved by many
lovely accommodation
lovely sight
low
low alcohol
low budget
low calorie
low cut
low fat
low interest
low interest rates
low key
low keyed
low level
low maintenance
low numbered edition
low overhead
low paying
low payment
low pressure
low profile
low rate
low rates
low risk
low start up cost
low strung
lowdown
lower
lower class
lower costs

lower income
lower your
lowest
lowest price
lowlife
loyal
loyal enthusiasts
loyal followers
loyal support
loyalty
lubricated
luck
lucky
lucky for you
lucrative
lucrative global business
lucrative industries
lucrative industry
lucrative Internet business
lucrative investment
lucrative line of products
lucrative partnerships
lucrative situation
lump sum
luscious
luscious colors
luxurious
luxurious accommodations
luxurious comfort
luxurious style
luxury
luxury of earning

Words & Phrases That Start With "M"

machine like
machine made
machine washable
mad about
made by
made in
made to order
made untold millions
magazine like
magazine mentioned
magenta colored
magic
magic formula
magic like
magical
magical remedy
magical scene
magically increase
magnet like
magnetic
magnificent
magnificent collection
magnificent color
magnificent future
magnificent ideas
magnificent treasure
mailing list tested
main goal is
maintain momentum
maintain rapport
maintain your current
maintained by
maintenance free
major
major announcement
major breakthrough
major cause
major commitment
major company

major corporations
major influence
major issue
major objectives
major priority
major wealth opportunity
majority of people
make $
make $ per hour
make $ per month
make $ per year
make (no) your investment
make (no)$ commission
make 100% commission
make a bundle
make a career change
make a fantastic living
make a fortune
make a fortune overnight
make a go of it
make a killing
make a living
make a long story short
make a lot of money
make a minimum of $
make a score
make additional income
make affiliate revenue
make as much money as you want
make at least $
make back (no) times your purchase
make believing
make extra income
make it big
make it happen
make it snappy
make maximum use of
make millions
make money

make money at home

make money at will

make money at your computer

make money online

make money your first day

make more money

make or break

make over

make people visit

make reoccurring income

make sales day and night

make short work of

make sure your

make the move

make them do your bidding

make thousands

make tons of money

make up to $ each week

make up your mind

make waves

make wheelbarrows of cash

make you rich

make yourself

make yourself a fortune

make yourself a home

making money

making money automatically

mall like

mammoth

mammoth collection

man like

man made

man sized

man slaughter

manage a team

manage your

manageable

managed by

management advice

management runned

mandatory

maneuver

maneuverability

manhandled

manifest your

manipulated by

manipulation proof

mankind

manual like

manufactured by

many ( ) have concluded that

many people

map like

maple flavored

marginal improvement

marginal return

markdown

marked down

market

market capacity

market demand

market downturn

market driven

market driven company

market identity

market leader

market moves

market niche

market oriented company

market penetration

market planning

market potential

market research

market risk

market saturation

market share

market value

marketability

marketed
marketing
marketing campaigns
marketing ethics
marketing etiquette
marketing help
marketing masters
marketing mix
marketing phenomena
marketing pioneers
marketing rights
marketing savvy
marketing success
marketing tools
markup
maroon colored
marquee
marriage like
marvelous design
marvelous opportunity
masculine
mashed
masked
mass
mass marketing
mass produced
massive
massive amounts of money
massive back end profits
massive collection
massive income
massive index
massive operation
massive reduction
massive supply
massive traffics floods
master
master reprint rights
master the art of

master your own destiny
mastermind
masterpiece
matched together
matchless perfection
matchless power
material like
maternal
mathematical
matter of fact
mature
mauve colored
maximize performance
maximize your money
maximized
maximum
maximum achievement
maximum effectiveness
maximum efficiency
maximum income potential
maximum results
maximum security
maximum strength
maybe you can finally
meal like
meaningful
meaningful benefits
meaningful investment
measurable
measurable results
measure the competition
measured
measures approximately
mechanical
medal of
media
media attention
media blitz
media goals

mediated by
medical
medicine like
medieval
medium
meet deadlines
meet me halfway
meeting friendly
mega earnings
mega traffic techniques
megabucks
mellow
melt away
melt the resistance
member
member of
member sign in
members only
membership site
memorabilia
memorable
memorable surprise
mentored by
mentoring program
menu like
merchandise
merchandised
merchant
merchant account
merger
mergers and acquisitions
merry
meshed together
mesmerize
mesmerize your customers
messed up
metal
metallic
metric

micro
microchip
microwavable
microwave safe
mid life
middle
middle class
middleman
midway
midweek
mighty
military
military backed
milk it for all it's worth
millennium
million dollar
million dollar secret
millions
millions of people want
millions of potential customers
mind blowing
mind boggling
mind busting
mind expanding
mind opening
mind rocking
mindful
mingled
mini
miniature
minimal
minimal instruction
minimal learning curve
minimal promotion
minimal resistant
minimize
minimize hassles
minimize returns
minimized

minimum
minimum effort
minimum supervision
minimum work
minor adjustment
minority owned
mint
mint condition
miracle
miraculous
mission statement
mistake proof
mistaken
mistakes to avoid
mixable
mixed
mixture like
mlm
mobile
modeled
modeled organization
moderate
moderate cost
moderated
modern
modern day
modern device
modern equipment
modernized
modest income
modifiable
modified
moist
mom and pop business
moment of truth
money
money back guarantee
money from home
money in record time

money is no object
money isn't everything
money just pours in
money less
money making concepts
money making ideas
money making opportunities
money making opportunity
money making robot
money making web site
money management
money on demand
money saving
money saving coupon
money talks
money vacuum
money well spent
money while you sleep
moneymaker
monitored
monopoly like
monster looking
monthly
monthly check
monthly royalties
monumental
monumental collection
morale
more bang for your buck
more clients than you can handle
more in less time
more than (no) hours of
more than (no) years
more than I ever expected
mortal like
mortgage
mortgage broker
most
most accessible

most advanced
most businesses know
most fail
most important investment
most overlooked
most prized
most trusted
mother of all
motherly
motivate
motivate prospects
motivate your affiliates
motivate your employees
motivated
motivation
motivational
motive driven
mountain of cash
mouth filling
mouth opening
mouth watering
mouth watering menu
movable
movers and shakers
much read
much used
multi colored
multi faceted
multi grade
multi million dollar
multi million dollar business
multi national corporations
multi user
multibrand strategy
multifunctional
multilevel selling
multimedia
multiple
multiple branding

multiple products to sell
multiple streams of income
multiplied
multiply your
multiply my efforts
multiply the results
multiply your influence
multiply your links
multiply your repeat sales
multiply your sales
municipal
mushroomed
musical
must attend event
must have
must read
must see
muted
mutual
mutual exceptions
mutual fund
mutual understanding
mutually
my (no) minute
my (no) part formula for
my actual pay check
my bank deposit
my best investment
my biggest complaint is
my first reaction was
my gut reaction is
my highest rating
my most cherish possessions
my name is
my only regret is
my overall rating is
my reputation is on the line
my sales by months
my secret sources for

my sure fire method
my very first day I made
mysterious
mystery like
mystic
mystical
myth like
mythical

Words & Phrases That Start With "N"

nail biting
nailed down
naked
naked truth
named the
nameless
narrow
narrow minded
nasty
nation wide
national
national craze
national treasure
nationally
nationwide
natural
natural born
natural color
natural finish
natural ingredients
natural quality
naturally you will
nature friendly
naughty
naughty secrets
navigated by
navigation
near miss
near perfect
near perfect achievement
near record
near you
neat
neato
necessary
necessary parts
necessary requirement
necessary tools
necessity

neck breaking
needs
need be
need I say more
needy
negative
negative cash flow
negotiable price
negotiate
negotiated
neighborly
neon
nerve racking
nest egg
net
net earnings
net income
net profits
net revenue
net sales
net worth
netiquette
netted over
network marketing
network of customers
network security
networked
networking like
never
never be laid off
never been released
never been removed from box
never ceases to amaze me
never cut corners again
never ending
never ending source
never ending stream of green
never ending supply
never ending traffic

never failing
never get ripped off
never have to deal with
never heard of information
never live pay check to pay check
never opened
never out dated
never pay a penny
never pay for advertising
never say never
never seen anything like it
never seen before
never seen before information
never shell out money
never struggle again
never throw away money again
never to be forgotten
never used in circulation
never wait for checks
never worry about
never worry about money again
new
new age
new and improved
new approach to business
new blood
new bread
new concept
new dimension
new economy
new found
new found wealth
new ground
new leads every week
new lease on life
new look
new order
new release
new standard

new style
new twist
new wave
new world
new year
newbie friendly
newbies
newer
newest
newest fad
newest information
newfound
newly
news
news break
news case
news clip
news group
news mentioned
news release
news room
news service
news sheet
newscast
newsworthiness
newsworthy
newsworthy event
next best
nice
nice distinction
niche
niche market
niche marketing
niche markets
nifty
night long
nightly
nimble
nine

nippy
nitty gritty
no
no 1
no ad budget
no additional charge
no additives
no advertising costs
no application fees
no b.s.
no better time to invest in
no better way
no bottom feeding
no brainer promotion
no clutter
no commute
no complicated
no complicated system
no computer needed
no contracts
no cost opportunity
no cost technique
no costly overhead
no costly repairs
no costly supplies
no credit check
no damage
no degree required
no distribution costs
no education required
no employee costs
no employees
no employees to manage
no expensive equipment
no experience
no experience needed
no extra cost
no face to face selling
no fault

no fighting morning traffic
no fillers included
no financial risk
no financial stress
no financial worry
no fluff
no fly by night scam
no fulfillment costs
no gimmicks
no guess work
no hands on work
no hard work
no hesitation saying
no hidden fees
no hidden reserve
no holds barred
no HTML knowledge
no hype
no interest
no Internet connection
no inventory
no inventory to ship
no investment
no large investment
no learning curve
no loans
no long term commitment
no maintenance
no matter how much you
no matter what business
no matter what you're selling
no matter where you live
no matter who you are
no meetings
no merchant account
no merchant account needed
no minimum
no misinformation
no money down

no money needed
no money to risk
no monthly charges
no more 9 to 5
no more being flat broke
no more endless searching
no more everyday grind
no more guess work
no more headaches
no more rejections
no more sleepless nights
no more stress
no more supervisors
no more time clock
no nonsense advice
no obligation
no on going fees
no operating costs
no or low overhead
no out dated information
no out of pocket expense
no out of pocket money
no packaging expenses
no pain no gain
no phone calls
no presentations
no previous experience
no product reproduction costs
no programming knowledge
no prospect can resist
no questions asked
no recycled information
no rehashed information
no rejection
no repairs
no reserves
no risk
no royalty fees
no same old information

no scam
no secretary
no selling
no set up fee
no shipping fees
no side effects
no sign up fees
no skills required
no software needed
no software to download
no special education
no sponsoring
no staff
no strings attached
no sweat
no technical ability
no technical knowledge
no time like the present
no time required
no win
no work on your part
noble
noble service
noble thought
noise proof
nonabrasive
nonacid
nonaddicting
nonaddictive
nonadditive
noncompetitive
nonconforming
nondisclosure
noneffective
nonessential
nonexplosive
nonfiction
nonfictional
nonflammable

nongovernment
nonhuman
nonindustrial
nonlethal
nonmandatory
nonpayment
nonprofessional
nonprofit
nonprofitable
nonrecurring
nonrenewable
nonresident
nonrestrictive
nonspecific
nonspillable
nonstick
nonstop
nonsurgical
nonverbal
nook and cranny
normal
nostalgic
nosy
not a fly by night scam
not a franchise
not a pyramid
not a scam
not by a long shot
not for everyone
not in a thousand years
not on your life
not refurbished
not to worry
not totally convinced yet
notability
notable
notable examples
noted by
noted expert

noteworthy
nothing comes close
nothing down
nothing to lose
nothing ventured, nothing gained
noticeable
noticeable adjustment
noticeable trend
noticed by
nourishing
novel
novel idea
novice friendly
now
now available
now for the first time you
now involved in
now is the time to get
now or never
now you can own
nuclear free
nude
nudity
null and void
number (no)
numeral like
numeric
numero uno
numerous
numerous examples
nurturing
nutrient rich
nutrients
nutrition like
nutritional
nutritional discovery
nuts and bolts
nutty

Words & Phrases That Start With "O"

oak
obese
objectionable
objective
obligated
obligation to
obliterate your competition
oblivious to
obscene
obscene amounts of cash
obscene profits
obsession like
obsessive over
obsolete
obtainable
obtainable money
obvious that
obvious urgency
obviously you can
occasional
occasionally customers
occupational
occurring commission
odd
odd looking
odds and ends
odor less
off and running
off beat
off center
off color
off duty
off key
off line
off road
off shore
off the books
off the shelf
off the wall

off to a running start
off year
offered by
official
official credentials
official guide
official version
officially
off-line
offset
offshore
oily
ok
old age
old fashion
old school
old schooled
old style
old time
old tradition
old world
older
oldest
oldie but goodie
on a scale of 1 to 10
on a shoestring budget
on a silver platter
on a tight budget
on automatic pilot
on cue
on easy street
on sale
on screen
on site repair
on target
on the blink of
on the money
on the right track
on the spot

on time
onboard
once and for all
once flourishing economy
once in a blue moon
once in a lifetime
once upon a time
once you own our product
one
one and only
one and the same
one comment from (name)
one day workshop
one dimensional
one in a million
one level
one of a kind
one of a kind collection
one of the best
one of the most
one of those rare products
one on one coaching
one on one mentoring
one owner
one person business
one shot deal
one sided
one simple
one size fits all
one source
one stop
one stop resource
one stop shopping
one sunny day
one time fee
one up
one way or another
ongoing
ongoing expansion

ongoing profits
ongoing training
online
online access
online auction
online campaign
online mall
online marketing
online or off-line
online ordering
online recruiting
online revenue
online sales process
online service
only ($) a month
only ($) a year
only ($) for a subscription
only ($) for instant access
only ($) for lifetime access
only (no) left
only (no) made
only a pinch
only for serious people
only investing ($) benefit
only investing ($) per chapter
only one click
only paying ($) per page
only paying ($) per word
only serious people apply
only spending ($) pay day
only spending ($) per tip
only the current information
only the tip of the iceberg
oodles of
open and shut
open book
open ended
open eye
open field

open invitation
open market
open minded
open their wallets
opening bid
operate you own business
operated
operating advantages
operating budget
operating costs
operating expenses
operational
operative
opinion friendly
opinionated
opportunist
opportunities open up
opportunity
opposition proof
optic
optical
optimal
optimal levels
optimize your time
optimized
optimum
optimum accuracy
optional
or you pay me nothing
orange
orchestrate your
orchestrated
order
order before (day,date,time)
order form free
order grabbing
order in the next
order now
order now and I'll include

order page
order processing
order pulling
order pulling copy
order ready web site
ordered by
orders keep pouring in
orders processed automatically
ordinary
organic
organization
organization to specialize in
organization wide
organize your
organized
organized table of contents
oriental
oriented
original
original creation
original mint
original production
originated
our clients say
out of date
out of pocket
out of pocket expensive
out of sight
out of the ordinary
out of this world
out perform
out produce
out source
outbreak of
outburst
outgoing
outgrow
outlandish
outlast

outline the benefits
outlined
outmaneuver
outnumber
outperform
outperform your competitors
output
outrage
outrageous
outrageous amount
outrageous profits
outrageously rich
outright sale
outscore
outsell
outsell the competition
outshine
outside
outsmart
outsmart your competition
outsourcing
outspend
outspoken
outstanding ability
outstanding credentials
outstanding merits
outstanding performance
outstanding qualities
outstanding quality
over $ my very first month
over (no) MB of information
over (no) pages of testimonials
over (no) searchable chapters
over (no) tactics
over and above
over looked
over powering
over the counter
over the past few years

over the past year
overactive
overall
overcome objections
overcome your
overcrowded
overdrive
overemphasis
overexcited about
overexposure
overflowing
overflowing profit
overhaul your
overhauled
overhead costs
overindulge
overjoyed
overlooked opportunities
overnight
overnight expert
overnight shipping
overnight success
overpowering effects
overrides on sales
overriding advantage
overriding benefit
oversized
oversold
overstate
overstocked
oversupply
overtake the competition
overtake your
overwhelmed by
overwhelming
overwhelming display
overwhelming force
overwhelming impression
overwhelming success

overwhelming tasks
overwhelming urge
overwhelming variety
overworked
owe yourself
own your own
owned by
owner of

Words & Phrases That Start With
"P"

pacesetter
package deal
package design
packaged and delivered
packaged goods
packaging friendly
packed
packed with
packs a punch
padded
padding included
paid every week
paid in full
paid up
pain free
pain killer
pain less
painful
painful process
painstaking
paint by numbers formula
paint the town red
painted
paired with
palace like
pales in comparison
palm sized
pamper yourself
pampered by
panel of experts
paper work free
paperless
paradise
parent friendly
parental guidance
part time
part time income
participate in
particular

partner with
partners world wide
partnership
party like
passed by
passion
passionate
passive
passive income stream
password
password and user name
password protected
password protection
password required
past customers
patched
patent pending
patience
patriotic
patrolled by
patterned
patterned after
paved
pay an arm and leg
pay as you go
pay bills on time
pay later
pay nothing
pay now
pay off
pay off your bills
pay off your credit cards
pay per click
pay per lead
pay per sale
pay per use
pay up now
pay your bills on time
payable

payable to

payday

paying benefits

paying bills before they're due

paying clients

payload

payment free

payment systems

payroll

pays dividends

pays dividends for years

pays for itself

pays on multiple levels

pays out fast

peace like

peace of minds

peaceful

peak at

peak efficiency

peak level

peak performance

peaked

peculiar looking

pending your order

penetrate their minds

penniless

penny pincher

pennyworth

people friendly

people from all over the world have bought it

people have paid up to $

people just like you

people pay $

peppermint flavored

peppery

perceived by

perceived value

percent of

perfect

perfect accent

perfect asset

perfect compliment

perfect condition

perfect detail

perfect fit

perfect ideas

perfect match

perfect size

perfect solution

perfect souvenir

perfect timing

perfected system

perfectible

perfection

perfectly legal

perfectly suited

performance tested

performed by

perhaps you're wondering

periodic discounts

periodical improvements

permanent

permanent commitment

permanent income

permanent influence

permanent monthly income

permanent relief

permanent satisfaction

permanent solution

permanently owned

permanently retire

perpetual income

perpetual promotional

perplexing phenomenon

persistence free

person friendly

person to person

personal	pictured by many as
personal fortune	pie in the sky
personal growth	piece of mind
personal insights	piece of the wealth
personal mentor	pierced by
personal promise	pig like
personal security	piggyback offer
personal selling	piggybacking
personalized	pile up
personalized list of	piles of cash
personally refund	pillar of success
persuade	pin down your
persuade anyone, anytime	pine scented
persuade buying decisions	pink colored
persuade people to spend	pinpoint achievement
persuade skeptical customers	pinpointed by
persuade your prospects	pins and needles
persuaded by	pint sized
persuasion like	pioneered
persuasive	pipe lined
pet friendly	piped in
petite	pitched
phased out	pitches in
phenomenal breakthrough	pivotal
phenomenal level	pivotal component
photograph of	pivotal decisions
photographed by	pivotal event
photos of	placed (no)th
physical	places to
physically changing	plagued by
physique	plain
pick and choose	plain and simple
pick up the pieces	plain truth
pick your	plan of action
picked by	planet like
pictorial	planetary
picture investing	planned
picture of	planned out
picture perfect	planning phrase

plant like
plant the seeds
planted by
plastic
plated with
platinum
play
play for keeps
play hardball
play it safe
playable
played by
playful
pleasant accent
pleasant sent
pleasing personality
pleasing results
pleasing sound
pleasurable
pleasure
pledge to
plow new ground
plucked from
plug in
plug in cash machine
plunge into
plural
plus
plus size
plush
pocket
pocket sized
pocket up to
poem like
poetic
point and click
point blank
point of purchase
pointless

poised for
poison free
poisoned
poker faced
polar
policed by
polished
polished looked
polished performer
polished skills
polished style
polite
political
politically correct
pollute less
polluted by
pollution proof
pool of experts
poor
poorer
poorest
pop up
popped
popular
popular acclaim
popular myth
popularity
popularized by
population accepted
portability
portable
portfolio
portion of
position yourself
positional
positioned by
positive
positive future
positive impact

positive influence
positive outlook
positively
posses every
posses knowledge of
possibilities are endless
possibly you should
post holiday
postage and handling
postage free
potent
potent force
potent influence
potential
potential bargain
potential benefits
potential demand
pounding
pouring money
pouring money down the drain
poverty proof
poverty stricken
powdered
power
power packed
powerful
powerful company
powerful impact
powerful incentive
powerful technology
powerhouse
powerless
practicable alternative
practical
practical benefits
practical choice
practical information
practical methods
practical solution

practically with no effort
practice free
practice what you preach
praised by
praiseworthy
prank proof
pre owned
pre publication opportunity
pre qualified
pre qualified customers
pre qualified traffic
pre release
pre sale
pre written
preached by many
prearrange
precious
precious asset
precious free time
precious opportunity
precise
precise adjustment
precise detail
precise function
precise standards
precise timing
precision
precision quality
preconception that
predator like
predatory
predetermine
predict
predict new trends
predictable
preemptive
preface driven
prefect tools
preferred by many

preferred member
prehistoric
premier
premier collection
premier offering
premium
prepaided
prepare to discover
prepared by
prepay now
prescription free
preselected
presell
presentable
presentation
presentational
presented by
preserve your
preserved
president
presidential like
press covered
press release sample
pressing issues of
prestige
prestigious organization
presuppose you ordered
pretend earning $
pretend your
pretty
pretty penny
prevention
preventive
previously released
price break
price conscious
price cutting
price friendly
price list

price points
price range
price reduction
price war
priced right
priceless
priceless help
priceless knowledge
priceless masterpiece
priceless opportunity
priceless treasure
pricing strategy
prickly
pride and joy
primary
prime earning
prime location
prime position
prime time
primed
primer on
primitive
principle and interest
print on demand
print out edition
printed
privacy
privacy policy
private
private broadcast
private consultation
private membership
private sector
private stock
privately funded
privately held
privileged
privileged access
prize appealing

prize winning
prized collection
prized institution
pro
proactive
proactive professional
proactive thinker
problem free
problem free delivery
problem laden
problem less
problem solved
processed by
proclaimed by many
procrastination proof
produced by
product
product class
product creation
product design
product development
product diversification
product driven
product empire
product life
product life cycle
product line
product mix
product package
product placement
product selling formulas
production
productive
productivity friendly
profession less
professional
professional advice
professional guidance
professional installed

professional looking
professional organization
professional product graphics
professional results
professional services
professional standards
professional teacher
professional trends
professional values
professional web site
professionally checked
professionally designed
proficiency
proficient
profile of
profiled by
profit
profit and loss
profit boosters
profit center
profit driven
profit for life
profit from
profit generating
profit levels
profit making
profit margin
profit model
profit motive
profit oriented
profit potential
profit producing
profit right away
profit sharing
profit system
profitability
profitable
profitable advice
profitable as possible

profitable asset
profitable business ideas
profitable firm
profitable formula
profitable information
profitable investment
profitable membership
profitable price
profitable product idea
profitable projects
profitable response
profitable strategies
profitable ventures
profits everyday
profits month after month
profits through the roof
profits with minimum risk
profound
profound impact
profound though
program their mind
programmable
programmed
programmer friendly
programming proof
progressive
prohibited
project friendly
projectable figures
projected by many
prolific
prolong use
prominent
promise the moon
promise you
promises I'll make you
promising company
promising future
promising ideas

promising outlook
promising solution
promising times
promo
promote
promote it in (no) minutes
promote your business
promote your site
promote yourself
promoted
promoted to
promoting any product
promotion
promotional
promotional phenomenon
promotional planning
promotional software
promotional tool
prompt action
prompt service
prompted by
promptly shipped
prone to
proof
proofread by
propaganda proof
propel
propel visitors
propel your traffic
proper
prophet like
proportional
proposal accepting
pros
pros and cons
prospect like
prospecting
prospective
prospective clients

prospects galore
prospects on demand
prospects to paying customers
prospects won't resist
prosper during a recession
prosper in bad times
prosperity
prosperous business
prosperous future
prosperous lifestyle
protect your business
protected by our
protection
protective
prototype
proudly presents
provable figures
prove it to yourself
prove your
proved
proven
proven and tested
proven effective
proven fact
proven in the field
proven leader
proven marketing system
proven name
proven performer
proven revenue models
proven solutions
proven step by step formula
proven to work
proven track record
proven ways
provided by
provided technical assistance to
provisional
psychedelic

psychological
public access
public policy
public relations
publicize your business
publicized
publicly held
published (date)
published by
publisher of
puffy
pull all the stops
pull in an additional $ this year
pull like crazy
pull more than $
pull your weight
pulled
pulling power
pulsating
pulverize the competition
punctual
punish proof
punk like
purchasable
purchase today
purchased by
pure
pure and simple
pure blooded
pure convenience
pure delight
pure fact
pure gold
pure luck
pure profit
purebred
purple colored
purposed by
push button

push the envelope
push the right buttons
push their hot bottoms
put down any about
put money on it
put two and two together
put up or shut up
put your money where you mouth is

Words & Phrases That Start With "Q"

quadruple profits
quadruple the results
quadruple your earnings
quadruple your sales
quake proof
qualified
qualified choice
qualified guide
qualified leads
qualified responses
qualified source
qualify prospects
qualify yourself
qualifying
quality
quality assurance
quality awareness
quality control
quality crafted
quality enhancing
quality management
quality materials
quality visitors
quantity driven
queen like
quenching
quest driven
question friendly
questionable
quick
quick break
quick buck
quick cash
quick change
quick decline
quick fire
quick fix
quick operation
quick recovery

quick reference
quick response
quick return
quick shifting
quick solution
quick tempered
quickest
quiet
quilted
quit feeling
quit making peanuts
quit your day job
quit your job
quite old
quiz like
quota driven
quotable
quoted by

Words & Phrases That Start With
"R"

racked to sell
radar like
radiant
radiant color
radiant future
radical approach
radical concept
radio like
rags to riches
rain or shine
raise eyebrows
raise the bar
raise your
raise your friend's eyebrows
raise your sights
raised to
raising this price to $
rake in
rake in an extra $
rake in over $
rake in the dough
rake in the profits
random
randomly selected
ranked as the
rant and rave
rapid action
rapid delivery
rapid fire
rapid growth potential
rare
rare craftsmanship
rare delight
rare design
rare find
rare formula
rare information
rare insights
rare moment

rare opportunity
rare pleasure
rare power
rarely
rarely seen
rarely used tactics
rarest ( ) that exists today
rat race
rate of growth
rate of return
rated by
rated number (no)
rational choice
rational purpose
rave reviews
raving fans
ravish
raw
razor
razor like
razor sharp
razzle dazzle
reaccept
reach a new milestone
reach for the sky
reach for your
reach new levels
reach your full potential
reach your goals
reachable dreams
reaction friendly
reactions from repeat customers
reactive
read below to learn
read between the lines
read our FAQ
read these endorsements
read these facts carefully
read these testimonials

read this jam packed
readable
readable dates
readable serial number
reader response
readers agree that
readers say
ready and able
ready and willing
ready made
ready to act prospects
ready to buy customers
ready to sell
ready to ship
ready to use
ready, willing and able
reaffirm your commitment to
real
real comfort
real freedom
real life examples
real secrets
real success
real time
real world
real world examples
real world experience
real world tested
realign your goals
realistic expectations
realistic ideas
realistic income
realistic objectives
reality
realize your potential
reap
reap the financial rewards
reap the rewards
reason to order

reasonable
reasonable price
reassert yourself as
reassure your
reassuring
reassuring answers
rebate
rebel like
rebuild your
recalculate
recall making
recall when
recapture your dreams
receipt provided
receptive to your offer
recession
recession busting
recession proof
recession resistant
recession wary
rechargeable
reciprocal
reciprocal links
reclaim your dreams
reclaim your freedom
recognizable brand
recognizable identity
recognize by many as
recognized expert
recommended by
recommended for professionals
recommit to
reconsider investing in
reconsolidate your
reconstructed with
record amount
record breaking
record breaking response rates
record breaking sales

record high
record year
recordable
recoup your investment
recyclable
red colored
red hot
red tap
redecorate your
redeem it at
redesigned as
redistributed by
reduce business costs
reduce charge backs and returns
reduce refunds
reduce the costs
reduce your
reduce your dependence
reduced
reduced material costs
reduced price
reevaluate your options
refer just (no) people
refer others
referable
reference like
referral
referral generating
referrals
referred as
refinance now
refined as
refinished
reflect back on buying
reflective
reformed
refreshed
refreshing
refreshing alternative

refreshing facts
refreshing news
refreshing taste
refund every penny
refund friendly
regained your
regardless of being
regardless of your education
regardless of your experience
regenerate your
regional
registered with
registration free
regular
regular communication
regulated by
reinforced
reinstated by
reinvent the wheel
reinventing the wheel
rejuvenate your
related to
relaxing
released today
reliable
reliable equipment
reliable expert
reliable guarantee
reliable promise
reliable source
reliable tracking
relief
remarkable
remarkable craftsmanship
remarkable information
remarkable performance
remarkable rates
remarkable story
remarkable timing

remedy the situation
remember having
remember when
remixed
remodeled
remote access
remote control
removable
remove buying defenses
remove life's obstacles
remove their objections
renegotiated
renew at only ($)
renew today
renewable
renewal free
renovated
rent free
rental
reoccurring income
reorder at a discount
reorganized package deal
repair free
repairable
repairs included
repeat customers
repeat sales
repeat traffic
repeat visitor
repeatable
replaceable
replaceable equipment
replaceable parts
replaced by
replacement parts
replay for free
replenish your
reply before (date)
report included

reported benefits
reprehensible
represented by
reprint rights
reproduced
reproduction rights
reprogram your
reputable
reputation is on the line
request our
requested by
required by law
requirements of
requires absolutely no
resale for
resale rights
research and development
researched
resell for profit
reseller package
reseller program
reserve before
reserve your copy
reserve your package
reserve your spot
reshape your
residence friendly
residential location
residual
residual benefits
residual checks
residual income
residual revenue stream
residual value
resistance free
resolvable problem
resource box
resourceful
respectable

respected authorities
respected by many as
respected genius
respected guru
respected representative
respond now
responds quickly
response is incredible
response rate
response required
responsibility
responsible
responsive to your
restock your
restored
restriction free
restrictive to
restructure your
restructured by
restyled
result proven
resulted in
resurging
retail
retain customers
retain more clients
retain more customers
retire
retire early
retire rich
retire young
retired by
retirement
retiring early
retroactive
retrospective
return friendly
return on investment
return on sales

return policies
returnable
returns
revamp your business
revamped
revealed
revealing
revealing details
reveals all
revenue
revenue bond
revenue enhancing
revenue generating
revenue month after month
revenue sharing
reverse your fortune
reversed
reversible
review our super
reviewed by
revisit soon
revitalized
revived
revolutionary
revolutionary information
reward employees
reward oriented
reward yourself
rewarded by
rewarding
rewarding challenge
rewarding industry
rich
rich accent
rich collection
rich color
rich detail
rich diversity
rich experience

rich flavor
rich menu
rich nutrient
richly detailed
richly textured
ridiculous
right
right and wrong
right at your finger tips
right away
right hand man
right handed
right thinking
rigorous
rigorous examination
rindy dink
rip roaring
ripe
ripe experience
ripped
ripped off
rise and fall
rise in costs
rise in sales
rising demand
risk free
risk proof
risk reversal
risk taker
risky
risky business
rival competition
river of cash
riveting
riveting package
road map to success
road to wealth
rob you of
robotic

robust
robust industry
rock bottom
rock bottom price
rock hard
rock solid
rocket launch your profits
rocket like
rocky
rocky times
roll out
romance
romantic
rookie friendly
rooting tooting
rotational
rough
rough edged
round
round table
rounded
rousing success
royal
royalties
royalty free
royalty free products
royalty free reprint rights
rub shoulders with
rugged
rugged tests
ruining your traffic
rule less
rules and guidelines to
run a home business
run around
run it from anywhere
run of the mill
run the show
running within hours

rural
rush delivery
rush hour
rush ordering
rust resistant
rusty

Words & Phrases That Start With
"S"

safe
safe investment
safeguarded
safety
safety requirements
said and done
salary driven
sale
sale of the century
saleable product
sales appeal
sales call
sales copy
sales driven
sales force
sales forecast
sales galore
sales generating
sales goal
sales intensifiers
sales letter
sales material
sales modifiers
sales over and over
sales pitch
sales process
sales promotion
sales pulling
sales quota
sales ratio
sales reps
sales stimulus
sales through the roof
salesman
salivate at
salty
same as
same as cash
same day

same old story
sample
samples of
sandy
sanitary
sassy
satisfaction
satisfactory
satisfied customers
satisfy your craving for
satisfying
satisfying pleasure
satisfying solutions
savable
save
save a small fortune
save a ton of money
save for college
save money
save thousands
save time
save your business
save yourself years of research
saves you from mistakes
saving time
savor
savvy
sawed off
scaled
scaled down
scandal proof
scarce
scare proof
scarf out
scented
schedule proven
scheduled
scheme proof
scholarly

school of
schooled by
scientific
scientific discovery
scientific fact
scientific material
scientific studies
scientifically tested
scientifically verified
scorching
screened by
scripted by
scrumptious
seal of approval
sealed air tight
seamless
search for
searing heat
seasonal
seasoned
seasoned pro
second
second income
second place
second rate
second to none
secondary
secondary market
secret
secret formula
secret recipe
secret selling blueprints
secret weapon
secretive
secrets of
secrets of the pros
secrets revealed
secrets to a successful
sectional

secure
secure a top spot
secure accommodations
secure investment
secure mail
secure ordering
secure ordering system
secure server
secured by
security
security measures
security policies
seduction
seductive appeal
seductive offer
see eye to eye
see for yourself
see it to believe it
see the light
see yourself selling
seed capital
seeded with
segmented
seize the day
seize the moment
seldom heard
seldom known
seldom used
select goods
select mixture
select winning products
selected from
self absorbing
self adjusting
self appointed
self assured
self centered
self cleaning
self confidence

self correcting
self development
self duplicating
self educated
self employed
self funding
self generating
self indulgence
self made millionaire
self mailer
self proclaimed
self reliant
self rising
self sufficient
self support
self supporting
self updating
self worth
sell
sell (no) and make back your money
sell a boatload
sell again and again
sell an unlimited number of copies
sell as many copies as you want
sell at warp speed
sell bucket loads of products
sell in hard times
sell like crazy
sell more by raising prices
sell or give away
sell out
sell products fast
sellable
seller's market
selling costs
selling experience
selling history
selling like crazy
selling like hot cakes

selling machine
selling multiple products
selling principles
selling skills
sells itself
semiautomatic
seminar like
semipro
senior
seniority chosen
sensational news
sensible agenda
sensible alternative
sensible choice
sensible ideas
sensible plan
sensible solution
sensitive intelligence
sensual
sentimental
separate
separate but equal
separate from the competition
separate winners from losers
separate yourself
separately
separates winners from losers
sequel
serge in
serial number
series of
serious
serious bids only
serious commitment
serious faced
serious minded
serious people only
serious profit potential
serious task at hand

seriously you can
served over (no)
service provider
serviceable
serviced (no)
seven
seven figure company
several (months, days, years) ago
sex
sexual
sexy
shake a leg
shameless
shameless pleasure
shape up or ship out
shape your prosperity
share of the market
shared by
shark like
sharp
sharp distinction
sharp increase
sharp insights
sharp tongued
sharper
sharpest
sheer pleasure
shelf life
shell out
shimmering
shining future
shinny
shipping included
shocked at
shocked at how cheap
shocking
shocking difference
shocking strategies
shoestring

shoestring budget
shop now
short
short cut
short lived
short order form
short range
short run
short sited
short term
shorted
shorten
shortly
show piece
show stopper
show the world
shredded
shrink resistant
sick and tried
sight unseen
sign of things to come
sign on
sign up
sign up instantly
signature free
signed and sealed
signed by ( )
signed, sealed and delivered
significant
significant acquisition
significant claims
silky
silly
silver colored
silver lining
simple
simple adjustment
simple approach
simple instructions

simple marketing system	skyrocket your profits
simple no cost ways	sky's the limit
simple plan	slash costs
simple pleasures	slashed
simple solution	sleazy
simple to follow outline	sleek
simple to use	slender
simplified	slice of the pie
simply explain	sliced
simultaneous	slick
simultaneously increase sales	slight accent
since the age of (no)	slim
sincere	slow
sincere desire	slow economy
single	slow growing
single edged	slow moving
sink or swim	slow poke
sink your teeth into	slow times
sit back and	slowdown
sit on your butt	sluggish economy
sit up and take notice	small
six	small business
six figure company	small company
six figure operation	small enough
six figure revenue	small fortune
sizable	small investment
sizable income	small minded
sizable portion	small package
size up	small size
sized right	small time
sized to fit	smaller
sizzling	smallest
skill	smallest ever
skilled	smart
skillful	smart decision
skillful maneuvers	smart money
skillfully managed	smart strategy
sky high income	smarter
skyrocket	smash hit

smash your competition
smashing success
smell the
smelly
smile because
smoke filled
smoke out
smoke proof
smoked
smoking
smooth
smooth adjustment
smooth feeling
smooth flavor
smooth spoken
smooth texture
smoothed
smoother
smothered in
snake like
sneak preview
sneaky
so called
so what
soaked in
soapy
soar your sales
soaring demand
soaring level
social
sodium free
soft
soft colors
soft market
soft sell
soft spoken
softened
softest
solar

sold
sold millions
sold out
sold thousands
solely
solid
solid angle
solid background
solid business
solid cash
solid choice
solid claims
solid commitment
solid credentials
solid firm
solid footing
solid foundation
solid gain
solid ground
solid information
solid investment
solid record
solid reputation
solid research
solid reward
solid study
solution
solve your cash flow problems
solve your problems
solved
solving a problem
some actual results of
some customers have told us
something for nothing
sooner or later
sooner the better
soothing
soothing scene
soothing sound

sophisticated
sophisticated equipment
sophisticated facility
sophisticated investor
sophisticated procedure
sophisticated tests
sore to new heights
sorted
sought after
sought after collection
sought after expert
sought after strategies
sound advice
sound alternative
sound investment
sound management
sound off
sound proof
sound strategies
sound workmanship
soupy
sour
souvenir
space age
spam free
spare no expense
spare parts
spare time
spark
spark your sales
sparkling
spearheaded
special
special alert
special edition
special gift
special pick
special rebate
special report

special touch
special training
specialist
specialize
specialized
specialized skills
specialty
specific
specific examples
specific mission
specifically
specifically designed
specified
spectacular
spectacular color
spectacular income
spectacular story
speechless
speed
speed up your success
speedy relief
speedy service
spellbound
spend time doing what you love
spend wisely
spending money
spending money without worry
spending spree
spent countless hours researching
spent time and money researching
spice up your
spicy
spiffy
spiked
spill my guts
spill over
spill their guts
spineless
spiral

spirit enhancing
spirited
spiritual
spiritual value
splendid
splendid color
splendid gift
splendid ideas
spliced
split run
split second
split up
spokesman said
sponsoring the
sponsorship
spontaneous
spoon fed
spoonful of
sport
sport utility
sporty
spotless perfection
spotlight
spotted
spread like wildfires
spread out
spreading
spreads like a
spring like
spring loaded
springboard your upsells
spruce up
square
squeaky
squeaky clean
squeezing your profits
squishing your sales
stability
stack the deck

staffed by
stage worthy
staged
staggering
staggering achievement
staggering figure
staggering findings
stained with
stainless steel
stampedes of traffic
stand alone products
stand by
stand out from the crowd
stand the test of time
stand up and be counted
standard
standard procedure
standardized
star crossed
star like
star studded
star studded event
starlight
starry eyed
start a dotcom business
start a thriving business
start earning today
start expanding
start from scratch
start making money in
start up
start up capital
start with little or no money
start with no money
start you own business
start your empire
starter kit
startling announcement
startling discovery

startling headline
startling truth
startlingly simple
startup costs
state approved
state of the art
state of the art facility
state of the art tests
statistical
statistical methods
stay ahead of competition
stay connected
stay in power
stay successful
stay up late
staying power
steadfast help
steady expansion
steady flow of subscribers
steady income
steal the show
steal the spotlight
stealth like
steam powered
steel
stenciled
step by step
step by step affiliate training
step by step directions
step by step instructions
step by step system
step up to the plate
sterile
sterilized
stern masterpiece
sticky
sticky sweet
stiff armed
stiff necked

still in package
still in the wrapper
stimulate your sales
stimulated
stimulating ideas
stomach filling
stomach turning
stop
stop hesitation
stop procrastinating
stop spending time searching for
stop the presses
stop wasting time with
stop what your doing
stop worrying
storable
stories of success
storms of leads
story book success
story like
story struck
straight
straight to the point information
straightforward
straightforward answers
straightforward technique
strange and unusual
strange phenomenon
strapped for cash
strategic
strategic partnerships
strategically maneuver
strategy
strawberry flavored
stream of referrals
streamed together
streaming
streamline
streamline your business

streamlined
streams of income
streams of traffic
street like
strength
strengthen your profits
strengthened
stress free
stress proof
stretch every dollar
stricken by
strict deadline
strictly confidential
strike gold
strike out
strike up a deal
strike while it's still hot
striking achievement
striking beauty
striking collections
striking design
striking difference
striking features
stripped
strive for perfection
strong
strong ability
strong arm
strong bonds of trust
strong close
strong commitments
strong consumer demand
strong credibility
strong demand
strong evidence
strong foundation
strong hold on
strong impact
strong interest

strong minded
strong skills
strong solution
strong willed
stronger
strongest
structural
structured
student friendly
studied submitted
studied tons of
studies prove that
study at home
stunning
stunning announcement
stunning presentations
stunning secrets
stunning sight
sturdy
sturdy materials
style conscious
styled with
subcontracted
subliminal
submerse yourself in
submitted by
subscribe now
subscribe to
subscriber log in
subscribing is easy
substance filled
substantial
substantial addition
substantial advantage
substantial benefits
substantial gain
substantial income
substantial increase
substantial wealth

substantially increase business
substantiated by
substituted with
succeed
succeed in a big way
succeed in business
succeed quickly
succeeded in
success
success and wealth
success oriented
success secrets
success stories
successful
successful analysis
successful antidote
successful at
successful company
successful corporation
successful firm
successful habits
successful talent
successfully follow up
successfully promote any product
sudden change in
sudden death
sudden economic change
sufficient
sufficient funding
suggested by
suggestions welcomed
suit and tie
suitable
summarized
summer like
super
super achiever
super affiliate
super bargain

super charge you profit
super efficient
super profitable
super strength
super successful
super swift
superb accommodations
superb condition
superb design
superb flavor
superb investment
superb miracle
superb performance
superb selection
superb view
supercharged
superficial
superhighway
superior
superior choice
superior location
superior methods
supernatural
supersensitive
superstar
supervised by
supplemented
supplied by
supplies limited
supply and demand
supply is limited
support friendly
support services
support systems
supported by
suppose you could just
supreme
supreme authority
sure fire

sure fire income
sure remedy
surely you will
surging business
surpass your goals
surpassed
surpassing beauty
surpassing elegance
surprise bonuses
surprise gift
surprising advantage
surprising amount
surprising answers
surprising collection
surprising information
surprising offer
surveyed by
survival proof
survive a slow economy
survive and prosper
sustainable
sustainable career
sweeping power
sweepstakes
sweet
sweet profits
sweet smelling
sweet sounding
sweet tasting
sweeten with
sweeter deal
swift
swift action
swift moving
swiftly flowing
swing into action
symbolic
symbolic value
sympathetic to your

synchronize your business
synchronized
synthetic
system like
systematic
systematic observation
systematic results

Words & Phrases That Start With
"T"

tabulate your order
tabulated by
tactics
tag team
tailor made
tailored
take a load off
take a look at all
take a peek
take a risk
take a shot
take advantage of
take all the
take apart
take care of business
take control of your life
take dream vacations
take it or leave it
take no prisoners
take orders in minutes
take orders instantly
take the plunge
take you by storm
take you by the hand
takes (no) minutes of your time
takes care of itself
takes full advantage of
takes the guess work out of
takes you step by step
talented
talented team of
talk of the Internet
talk of the town
tall
taller
tallest
tamed
tamper proof
tan colored

tantalize your senses
tantalizing
tantalizing facts
tantalizing mixture
tantalizing taste
tap into the
tapered
target audience
target market
target other potential markets
target price
targeted
targeted exposure
targeted traffic
tasteful
tasteful color
tastes like
tax advantage
tax benefits
tax deductible
tax exempt
tax free
tax free money
tax incentive
tax savings
team building
team like
team of experts
team up with
team work
tearjerker
technical
technical help
technology
technology sensitive industry
technology training
teeth chattering
teeth grinding
teeth jarring

tempting menu
tempting offer
tender
terms of sale
terrific
territorial
test drive
test everything automatically
test the waters
tested
tested marketing system
tested techniques
testimonials
thank you
thank you for checking out this
that's how good it is
that's just what you need
the (#no)
the (#no) best
the (no) elements every
the (no) ingredients
the (no) laws of
the (no) priorities of
the (no) steps
the (no) things you
the absolute best way
the actual ( ) I used to
the advantages of owning
the best of both worlds
the best thing since
the big problem with
the biggest names in
the biggest problem with
the bus stops here
the clock is ticking
the complete authority on
the complete guide to
the comprehensive guide to
the countdown begins

the country's top
the critical information
the difference between
the disadvantages of not
the easiest way
the exact steps
the fact is
the fail safe way to
the fastest method of
the fastest way
the final countdown
the first thing
the following is just
the following rewards
the going value
the grand master of
the hidden secrets
the hidden truth
the impossible dream
the inside story
the key is knowing how to
the latest information
the little known
the location of
the major highlights of
the mechanics of
the most important thing
the nation's foremost authority
the next level
the nuts and bolts of
the one mistake you
the one specific
the only ( ) like it
the only ( ) you'll need
the only game in town
the original sells for ($)
the parts of a
the perfect business
the pitfalls and mistakes of

the powerful advantages
the pros and cons
the proven
the question is
the real deal
the real keys to
the real reasons
the real thing
the risk is on me
the run down on
the safe route
the safe way to
the secret weapon
the secrets behind
the shocking truth
the simple question
the simple technique
the single most
the success you dream
the surprising facts
the thing that impressed me
the things you'll receive
the time is now
the time is right
the top (no) most
the topics included are
the truth about
the truth is
the very first thing
the whole shebang
the whole works
the word is out about
theft proof
there are a lot of myths about
there are very few people
there is no better time
there is nothing quite like
there is nothing wrong with
there's is nothing to it

there's never been a better time to
there's no free lunch
there's no tomorrow
there's no turning back
there's no where else to go
thermal
thermal lined
they have outdone their self
thick
thickest
thin
think about
think about spending
think of it as your personal
thinner
third
third class
third degree
third dimension
third place
third rate
thirst quenching
this ( ) has just about all the
this ( ) is for
this fact is supported by
this fact is verified by
this is no gimmick
this is the complete
this probably comes as no big surprise
thorough
thorough analysis
thorough knowledge
thorough process
thoroughly inspected
thoroughly researched
thought out
thought stopping
thousands

thousands of extra dollars
three
three dimensional
three easy payments of $
three time looser
threw thick and thin
thrifty
thrilling news
thrilling results
thrilling secrets
thrive in a bad economy
thriving industry
thriving market
throw away
ticket to success
ticky tacky
tidy
tight
tight cut
tight deadline
tight hold
tight lipped
tight security
tightwad
tilt the odds in your favor
time bomb
time clock
time consuming
time efficient ways
time honored
time honored custom
time honored solution
time is money
time is of the essence
time is running out
time released
time saving
time saving device
time saving ideas

time tested
timeless
timeless appeal
timeless classic
timeless gift
timeless masterpiece
timely help
timely ideas
timely information
timing is everything
tinted
tiny
tip of the iceberg
tip the scales
tip top shape
tire burning
tire spinning
titanic energy
to die for
to summarize
to the fullest
to the max
toll free
tongue hanging
tongue tied
tongue wagging
tons of marketing tools
too hot to handle
took (no) hours to create this
took me two seconds to decide
took me years to research
tool like
toolbox like
top
top achievers
top corporate giants
top dog
top dollar
top executives

top experts
top flight
top level
top marketing experts
top notch
top placement
top priority
top prize
top producing
top quality
top rated
top recruiters
top sales producer
top secret
top selling
topic driven
total comfort
total freedom
total satisfaction
total secrecy
total transformation
total winner
totally confidential
totally untouched
trade secrets
tradition bound
traditional
traditional approach
traffic building techniques
traffic growth
trail blazing
trained by
training system
transferable
transformed into
transportable
traveled
treasure
treasure chest

treasure map
treasured by
treasured forever
treatable
tremendous
tremendous amount
tremendous asset
tremendous bargain
tremendous breakthrough
tremendous experience
tremendous help
tremendous impact
tremendous profits
tremendous satisfaction
trendy design
trial
trial and error
trial offer
trial size
tricks of the trade
tried and true
trillion
triple crown
triple play
triple sales
tripled
triumphal announcement
trouble free
trouble free delivery
trouble shooting help
troubleshooting
truck loads of cash
truck loads of leads
true collectors piece
true facts
true financial security
true life
true story
trust me you have to

trusted
trustworthy
truthful
try it, you'll like it
turbo boost
turbo boost your sales
turn around your business
turn nothing into something
turn over a new leaf
turn your dream into a reality
turned on
TV mentioned
twisted
two for the price of one
two level
two sided
two tier
two way
two way street
two wheeled
tycoon

Words & Phrases That Start With
"U"

ultimate authority
ultimate collection of
ultimate gift
ultimate independence
ultimate time saver
umpteen
unbeatable offer
unbeatable price
unbelievable invention
unblemished reputation
unbounded energy
unbridled energy
unbridled enthusiasm
uncanny intelligence
uncensored
uncensored media
unclaimed fortune
unclaimed treasure
uncommon
uncommon information
uncommon techniques
uncontrollable urge
uncover
uncover a faster method
uncover insider techniques
uncover the
uncover uncommon
uncovered by
uncut
uncut version
undeniable evidence
under adverse conditions
under aged
under close scrutiny
under cut
under priced
under privileged
under the gun
under the table

under utilized
underground
underground economy
understand the importance of
underutilized asset
undetectable sales boosters
undreamed of
unearth gold
unearth more profits
unedited
unfair advantage
unfair competition
unfathomed secrets
unforgettable
unforgettable experience
unforgettable impression
unheard of
unheard of level
unherald prosperity
unimaginable
unimaginable luxury
unique
unique antique
unique blend
unique concept
unique methods
unique moment
unique opportunity
unique policy
unique qualifications
unique selling point
unique status
unique visits
uniquely qualified
united
universal
universal acclaim
universal phenomenon
universal recognition

unleaded
unleash
unleash the power of
unleashed
unless you already know
unlike any other
unlike anything
unlike anything you've seen before
unlimited
unlimited access
unlimited budget
unlimited demand
unlimited fortune
unlimited innovation
unlimited potential
unlimited profit producers
unlimited resources
unlimited uses
unlimited wealth
unmarked
unmatched
unnecessary paperwork
unofficial guide
unordinary
unorthodox
unorthodox methods
unparalleled success
unpreceded
unquestionable proof
unquestioned
unquestioned honesty
unquestioned originality
unquestioning trust
unreal
unrelenting formula
unrestricted access
unspoken
unspoken advice
unstoppable

unsung hero
unsurpassable
unsurpassed
unsurpassed perfection
unsurpassed reputation
untainted
untapped
untapped market
untapped opportunities
untapped resources
untapped wealth
untarnished
untarnished reputation
untaxed
unthinkable
untold
untold fortunes
untold riches
untold wealth
untouchable
untraceable
unused condition
unusual
unusual for me to endorse a product
unusual information
unusual insights
unusual phenomenon
up and coming
up for grabs
up sell
up the ante
up the corporate ladder
up to date
up to date data
up to date information
up to date methods
up to date on the latest
up to speed
up to the minute

up to the minute updates
upbeat
updated
updated weekly
upgrade
upgrade your business
upgraded
upholstered
upline
upper class
ups and downs
upscale
urban
urgency
urgent
urgent action
usable
useful
useful gifts
useful information
useful purpose
useful searching
useful tools
user friendly
utility
utilized by
utmost urgency

Words & Phrases That Start With
"V"

vacancy
vacant
vacation anytime
vacation money
vacuum packed
vaguely mentioned
valid
valid methods
valid proof
valid threat
validated by
valuable
valuable addition
valuable asset
valuable collection
valuable coupon
valuable information
valuable insights
valuable knowledge
valuable resources
valuable service
value added
value added service
value conscious
value driven
valued by
vandal proof
vanilla flavored
vanishes instantly
vanishing
vanishing formula
vaporizing
variable climates
variable cost
variable expenses
varied
variety
various choices
varnished

varying styles
vast amount
vast asset
vast compilation
vast examples
vast industry
vast sums of
vaulted to number (no)
velvet covered
vender friendly
ventilated
venture capital
verbal warning
verbalized
verdict driven
verified by
versatile
vertical
very good condition
very good shape
very light
very proficient
veteran like
veto proof
vetoed
vibrant colors
vibrant display
vibrating
victim less
victorious
videotaped
view yourself
viewable
viewpoint
vigilant
vigorous training
villain like
vindicated
vintage

vintage craftsmanship
vintage year
violet colored
viral
viral marketing
virtual assistant
virtual presence
virtual reality
virtual storefront
virtually no cost
virtually zero risk
virus like
visibility
visible plan
visioned by
visit
visited by
visitor friendly
visitor to sales ratio
visitor tracking
visual control
visual less
visualize buying
visualize yourself
vital
vital agreement
vital component
vital force
vital function
vital help
vital issue
vital mission
vital parts
vital process
vital support
vivid
vivid accent
vivid color
vivid design

vivid detail
vivid reminder
vocal less
vocational
voice cracking
voice less
voiced their opinion
voided
volcanic
voltage
volume proof
volume resistance
voluntary
volunteering
voucher friendly
vow to
vulnerability
vulnerable
vulture like
vying for

Words & Phrases That Start With "W"

wacky
wads of cash
wage less
wage war
wager your
waist high
wait and see
wake up anytime
wake up call
wake up late
wallet opening
want more proof
war like
warehousing
warm
warm colors
warm hearted
warning
warp speed
warrant
warrant a pay check
warranty
was I surprised
wasteful
water boiling
water proof
water steaming
watered down
wave of the future
way back in (year)
way the ball bounces
ways and means
ways to use the
we aim to please
we do all the work
we do all the work for you
we guarantee you'll
we have all heard about
we process all orders

we reserve the right to
we spilled the beans
we take the orders
we will foot the bill
we will show you
weak
weak market
weak willed
weaker
weakest
wealth
wealth building
wealth multiplying strategies
wealth of information
wealthy
wealthy mindset
wear what you want
weathered
web
web designed
web hosted
web master
web page
web site
web site award
web site marketing
web traffic
weekends off
weekly freedom
weeknights off
weighed
weighs approximately
weighs in at
weird
welcomed to
well
well advanced
well advised
well balanced

well being
well beloved
well bred
well built
well chosen
well connected
well constructed
well crafted
well documented
well dressed
well educated
well established
well established company
well established institution
well favored
well groomed
well guarded
well informed
well kept secret
well known
well known figure
well liked
well made
well marked
well off
well oiled
well organized
well planned
well preserved
well qualified prospects
well regulated
well rounded
well set
well spoken
well stocked
well thought out
well thought out strategy
well to do
well trained

well worked
well worn
well worth the price
well worth what I paid
well written
wet
we've been online for (no)
we've sold (no) copies
what (customer) said
what a deal
what are you waiting for
what could
what do you
what does it mean to
what every person
what have you got to lose
what I am about to share
what I have to tell you
what if I told you
what if someone said to you
what if you could finally
what I'm about to
what I'm about to show you is
what I'm about to tell you is
what impressed me the most
what it takes to
what others are saying
what the doctored ordered
what the experts are saying
what to do when
what type of
what would an extra
what would you do if
what you need to know
what you should
what you've been looking for
what you'll discover
what you'll get
what you'll receive

what...?
wheel and deal
wheeler dealer
when I first started out in
when will you
when you order by
when you order today
when...?
where to find
where to get a
whether you're looking to
which of the
which...?
while you are sleeping
while you're on vacation
whinny
white collar
white colored
whiten
whiz
who...?
whole new ball game
wholesale price
wholesome advice
whopping
whopping increase
whopping success
why (no)% of businesses fail
why being an
why creating a
why I'm a expert
why is
why most
why people are
why people buy
why some people
why you can be
why you must get
why you must use

why you need
why you should never
why you should trust me
why you shouldn't
why you've got to
why...?
wicked
wide
wide availability
wide awake
wide distribution
wide implications
wide open
wide open market
wide range of products
wide ranging
wide selection
wide spectrum
wide variety
widened your
widespread
wild
wild extravaganza
wild success
wildly profitable
will go over big
will make a great gift
will make or break you
will never be leased
will never be rented
will never be sold
will pay for its self
will pay for your purchase
will stretch your mind
will supply you with
will work for you
win
win out
win some lose some

win their mind
win them over
win/win deal
win/win offer
win/win situation
winning ad
winning edge
winning ideas
winning personality
winning products
winning solution
winning strategies
wired
wireless
wisdom
wise advice
wise choice
wise investment
wish it was available sooner
wish like
wish list
wishful
wishy washy
with a added bonus
with flying colors
with handwritten letter
with little effort
with no start up money
with our product you can
with serial number
withdraw this offer at anytime
within minutes from now
without a big investment
without all the hype
without any of the frustration
without any of the hassle
without any of the stress
without any string attached
without any work

without breaking a sweat
without effort
without failing
without investing money
without investing time
without paying outrageous fees
without raising a figure
without spanning
without spending a fortune
without spending one red cent
without working hard
without working harder
withstand a slow economy
witty
woman like
won over
wonderful
wonderful organization
wonderful selection
wonderful sight
wondrous
won't be here tomorrow
word of mouth
words can't describe
words of wisdom
work a few hours a week
work at home
work at home on your computer
work for yourself
work free
work from home
work from your basement
work from your bedroom
work from your kitchen
work from your living room
work in your bathrobe
work in your pajamas
work in your sweats
work in your underwear

work less
work loaded
work of art
work smarter not harder
work the hours you want
work were you wish
work while you travel
work with
workable
workable ideas
workable objectives
workable plan
workaholic
worked by
worked closely with
working for
working from home
working less
working relationship
works every time
works like crazy
world class
world class faculty
world class standard
world class status
world famous
world renowned
world shaking
world wide
world wide phenomenon
world wide reputation
world wide web
world's largest
world's leading experts
world's oldest
worldwide recognition
worn down
worn out
worry free

worry free investment
worry free retirement
worst case scenario
worst ever
worth a fortune
worth a hundred times the cost
worth every
worth every dollar I spent
worth gold
worth it's weight in gold
worth over $
worth substantial sums
worth the price and then some
worthwhile
worthwhile cause
worthwhile charity
worthy acquisition
worthy addition
worthy of
worthy purpose
would be crazy not to buy
would you
would you like to
wouldn't you like to
woven with
wow your prospects
wrapped
wrapped with
wrinkle free
write it off
write you a blank check
write your own check
written for today's
written guarantee
written in everyday language
written in plain English
written so a baby could understand
it

Words & Phrases That Start With "X"

No words or phrases to provide for this section.

Words & Phrases That Start With
"Y"

yard long
year end
year in year out
year round
yearly
yearning for
years of experience
years of research
years practical experience
yellow colored
yes
you ain't seen nothing
you already recognize
you are about to discover how to
you are about to realize
you better believe it
you can do this
you can literally start
you can own my brain for
you can't possibly lose
you can't afford
you can't fail
you can't lose
you do not need experience to
you don't have
you don't have to be an expert
you don't know it yet
you don't need
you get
you have a
you have no risk
you have nothing to lose
you have to start here
you just have to see it
you know all those people who
you know that you
you may have already heard
you may realize you
you may want to

you might be thinking
you might want to
you never have to
you never know
you only need to do
you owe it to yourself
you probably feel
you will also receive
you will be
you will have learned
you won't find this in (location)
you won't have to
you won't see this everywhere
you'll be sorry
you'll discover
you'll find out
you'll get (no) bonuses
you'll get instant access
you'll get unlimited
you'll have a great reputation
you'll improve your
you'll know
you'll learn
you'll learn it all
you'll never find a better way to
you'll sell a ton of them
you'll treasure this
young
your crazy not to invest
your ethical duty
your moral duty
your not alone
your only paying $
your very own product
you're a creative marketer
you're a intelligent person
you're a skilled webmaster
you're a smart person
you're a talented entrepreneur

you're a wise investor
you're about to uncover
you're asking yourself
you're going to get
you're likely thinking
you're on the clock
you're probably tired
you're right on the money
yours for no charge
yours for the taking
youth like
youthful
you've probably heard

Words & Phrases That Start With "Z"

zapped
zero advertising budget
zero based
zero delivery cost
zero growth
zero in on
zero install
zero to implement
zestful
zesty
zig zagged
zilch
zillion
zipped
zoned by
zoo like

Index

abandon, 101
abiding, 98
ability, 20, 22, 50, 57, 58, 86, 115, 121, 155
able, 17, 139
abnormal, 17
about, 3, 19, 21, 46, 50, 54, 58, 65, 84, 85, 91, 92, 96, 99, 104, 113, 121, 133, 162, 176, 177, 184, 185
above, 16, 17, 121
abreast, 17, 96
abridged, 17
abrupt, 17
absolute, 16, 17, 20, 161
absolutely, 81, 85, 91, 141
absorbable, 17
absorbing, 17, 19, 147
abstracted, 17
abundance, 63
abundant, 17
academic, 17
academy, 17
accelerate, 17
accelerated, 17
accent, 64, 125, 127, 142, 150, 173
accented, 17
accept, 17
accepted, 17, 41, 127
accepting, 131
access, 10, 17, 49, 54, 59, 62, 66, 71, 77, 86, 89, 90, 100, 119, 129, 132, 141, 169, 184
accessible, 17, 108
accessories, 17
accident, 17
accidental, 17
acclaim, 41, 89, 90, 127, 168
acclaimed, 17, 41, 79
accommodation, 102

accommodations, 19, 37, 102, 147, 156
accompanied, 17
accomplish, 17
accomplished, 17
accomplishing, 17
according, 17
account, 88, 96, 107, 114
accountability, 17
accountable, 17
accountant, 17
accounted, 17
accounting, 40
accounts, 60
accuracy, 17, 39, 60, 120
accurate, 17
accused, 17
ace, 17
achieve, 17
achievement, 78, 106, 112, 126, 153, 155
achiever, 72, 156
achievers, 163
achieving, 17
acknowledged, 17
acknowledgment, 17
acknowledgments, 72, 73
acquire, 17
acquired, 17
acquisition, 149, 180
acquisitions, 107
acrobatic, 17
across, 71
act, 17, 18, 96, 139
action, 20, 49, 64, 86, 100, 126, 131, 138, 157, 170
activate, 18
activated, 18
activation, 18

active, 18
actor, 18
actress, 18
actual, 18, 78, 109, 151, 161
actually, 81, 91
ad, 18, 66, 67, 114, 179
adapt, 18
adaptable, 18
adaptive, 18
add, 18, 54, 81
added, 18, 172, 179
addict, 18
addicted, 18
addiction, 18
addictive, 18
adding, 20
addition, 16, 86, 101, 155, 172, 180
additional, 18, 54, 104, 114, 132
additive, 18
additives, 114
address, 18
addressed, 18
adequate, 18
adhered, 18
adhesive, 18
adjoin, 18
adjust, 18
adjusted, 18
adjuster, 22
adjusting, 147
adjustment, 73, 108, 116, 128, 149,
151
administer, 18
administrated, 18
administrator, 18
admirable, 18
admirer, 18
admissible, 18
admit, 18

adoptive, 18
adorable, 18
adore, 18
adrenaline, 18
ads, 41
adsorbing, 18
adult, 18
advance, 18
advanced, 4, 18, 27, 109, 176
advantage, 18, 21, 38, 47, 50, 51,
70, 121, 155, 157, 160, 168
advantageous, 18
advantages, 120, 161, 162
adventure, 18, 57, 59, 62, 73, 90
adverse, 18, 168
advertise, 18, 20
advertised, 18
advertisement, 18
advertising, 8, 18, 20, 38, 40, 60,
66, 71, 113, 114, 188
advice, 18, 26, 27, 36, 39, 51, 60,
63, 67, 71, 73, 77, 89, 91, 99, 105,
115, 130, 152, 169, 178, 179
advisable, 18
advise, 18
advised, 19, 50, 85, 176
advisor, 63
advocated, 19
aerial, 19
affected, 19
affection, 19
affectionate, 19
affiliate, 10, 14, 19, 26, 31, 42, 78,
87, 88, 94, 104, 154, 156
affiliates, 100, 109
affiliation, 19
affirm, 19
affirmations, 19
affirmative, 19

affix, 19
affluent, 19
afford, 19, 184
affordable, 19, 47
afraid, 19
after, 19, 86, 124, 131, 142, 152
afternoon, 73
again, 4, 29, 32, 81, 84, 112, 113, 148
against, 19, 74
age, 19, 20, 22, 87, 113, 118, 150, 152
aged, 168
agenda, 19, 78, 148
agent, 19
ago, 10, 149
agony, 19
agree, 19, 21, 59, 84, 85, 139
agreed, 19
agreement, 19, 27, 100, 173
ahead, 19, 29, 37, 96, 100, 154
aide, 4, 5
aided, 19
aim, 19, 176
aiming, 19
ain, 184
air, 16, 19, 147
airborne, 19
alarmed, 19
alarming, 19
alcohol, 102
alert, 55, 152
alien, 19
alienated, 19
aligned, 19
alignment, 19
alive, 19
all, 16, 17, 19, 20, 37, 39, 40, 55, 59, 64, 71, 91, 99, 107, 109, 119, 125, 132, 142, 160, 162, 176, 179, 184
allergy, 20
alley, 26
alliance, 20, 31
alliances, 31
allocated, 20
allow, 20
allowance, 18, 20
allowed, 20, 92
alluring, 20
almighty, 20
almost, 20, 84, 92
alone, 36, 153, 184
along, 72
alphabetized, 5
already, 32, 84, 169, 184
also, 5, 85, 184
altar, 20
altered, 20
alternated, 20
alternating, 20
alternative, 20, 21, 76, 94, 128, 140, 148, 152
alternatives, 39, 41
always, 20, 58, 81
am, 84, 177
amaze, 112
amazed, 20, 85
amazement, 20
amazing, 20
amazingly, 20
ambition, 20
ambitious, 20, 79
amended, 20
ammunition, 20
Amount, 1, 7
amount, 20, 37, 50, 82, 88, 90, 98, 121, 139, 157, 164, 172

amounts, 89, 106, 118
amphibious, 20
amplified, 20
amplify, 20
amusement, 20
amusing, 20
an, 4, 20, 26, 27, 31, 54, 70, 71, 72, 77, 81, 124, 132, 138, 148, 177, 178, 184
analysis, 20, 40, 48, 87, 156, 162
analyzed, 20
ancestor, 20
ancestral, 20
ancestry, 20
anchor, 21
ancient, 21
and, 3, 4, 5, 10, 16, 17, 19, 20, 26, 27, 28, 29, 30, 32, 35, 37, 41, 42, 50, 51, 54, 55, 62, 63, 64, 65, 66, 67, 70, 72, 73, 78, 80, 82, 87, 89, 91, 94, 99, 100, 101, 102, 105, 107, 108, 109, 113, 116, 118, 119, 120, 121, 124, 126, 127, 128, 129, 130, 131, 132, 133, 138, 139, 140, 141, 143, 146, 148, 149, 150, 152, 153, 154, 156, 157, 161, 162, 163, 164, 169, 170, 176, 178, 180
angel, 20, 21, 74
anger, 21
angered, 21
angle, 151
angled, 21
anguish, 21
animal, 21
animated, 21
ankle, 21
anniversary, 21
announcement, 88, 98, 104, 153, 155, 164

annoyance, 21
annoyed, 21
annoying, 21
annual, 21
anonymous, 21
another, 18, 51, 91, 119
answerable, 21
answered, 21
answering, 21
answers, 21, 36, 42, 47, 85, 139, 154, 157
ante, 169
anti, 21
anticipated, 21, 54
antidote, 156
antique, 21, 23, 58, 64, 168
any, 21, 27, 40, 49, 51, 65, 131, 133, 156, 169, 179
anybody, 21
anyhow, 21
anyone, 21, 50, 80, 126
anyplace, 21
anything, 21, 32, 50, 62, 85, 113, 169
anytime, 21, 34, 88, 126, 172, 176, 179
anyway, 21
anywhere, 21, 77, 79, 143
apart, 21, 29, 160
apologetic, 21
apology, 21
apparent, 21
appeal, 21, 55, 76, 77, 86, 91, 146, 147, 163
appealing, 21, 90, 129
appearance, 21
appliance, 21
applicable, 21
application, 21, 114

apply, 119
appointed, 21, 147
appraisal, 21
appraised, 21
appreciate, 21, 84
apprentice, 21
approach, 16, 39, 55, 76, 89, 113, 138, 149, 164
approachable, 21
appropriate, 21
approval, 21, 147
approved, 21, 50, 154
approximat, 21
approximately, 106, 176
archive, 16, 21
are, 4, 5, 21, 42, 78, 84, 114, 128, 162, 177, 178, 184
area, 86
aren, 84
arm, 20, 21, 124, 155
armed, 21, 77, 154
around, 21, 23, 31, 71, 94, 143, 165
arousing, 21
arranged, 5, 22
arrangement, 16
array, 22
arsenal, 4, 16
art, 22, 106, 154, 180
article, 22, 87
articles, 66
articulate, 79
artifact, 22
artificial, 22
artist, 22
As, 5
as, 22, 31, 50, 54, 55, 58, 59, 60, 67, 73, 104, 124, 126, 130, 138, 139, 140, 142, 146, 148, 162
ask, 22, 50

asked, 77, 115
asking, 22, 185
aspects, 59
assassin, 22
assembled, 22, 68
assembles, 22
assembly, 22
assert, 22
assess, 22
assessable, 22
assessed, 22
asset, 22, 125, 128, 131, 164, 168, 172
assigned, 22
assist, 4
assistance, 132
assistant, 173
assisted, 39
assists, 22
Associate, 46
associate, 22, 27
association, 22
assumable, 22
assume, 22, 85
assumed, 22
assurance, 136
assure, 22
assured, 22, 147
astonishing, 22
astounding, 22
astronomical, 20, 22
at, 4, 10, 18, 19, 22, 34, 36, 37, 41, 59, 63, 71, 73, 80, 84, 101, 102, 104, 105, 125, 140, 141, 143, 146, 148, 149, 155, 156, 160, 176, 179
athlete, 22
athletic, 22
atmosphere, 90
atomic, 22

attached, 115, 179
attachments, 22
attain, 22
attainable, 22
attempt, 22
attend, 22, 109
attention, 22, 71, 73, 80, 90, 106
attentive, 22
attest, 22
attitude, 22
attract, 22
attracting, 22, 36
attractive, 22
Auction, 46
auction, 22, 119
audible, 22
audience, 54, 160
audio, 22
audit, 22
augmented, 22
authentic, 22, 23
authentication, 23
author, 23, 37
authored, 23, 37
authoring, 23
authoritative, 23
authorities, 142
authority, 23, 38, 58, 70, 77, 156, 161, 168
authorization, 23
authorized, 23
auto, 23, 71
autographed, 23
automate, 23
automated, 23, 68
automatic, 23, 118
automatically, 23, 81, 105, 120, 161
automating, 23
automation, 23

autosuggestibility, 23
availability, 23, 100, 178
available, 23, 116, 179
avalanche, 23
avenues, 5
average, 17, 23, 27, 88
avid, 23
avoid, 23, 81, 108
awaited, 101
awake, 178
award, 23, 176
awarded, 23
awards, 39
awareness, 136
away, 29, 30, 50, 71, 72, 84, 107, 113, 130, 143, 148, 163
awe, 23
awed, 23
awesome, 23
awful, 23
awhile, 23
babe, 26
baby, 26, 180
back, 5, 23, 26, 30, 34, 38, 51, 62, 71, 72, 84, 94, 98, 104, 106, 108, 140, 148, 150, 162, 176
backdoor, 26
backed, 26, 107
background, 17, 26, 50, 151
backlash, 26
backlogged, 26
backs, 140
bacon, 30
bad, 26, 132, 163
bag, 26, 87
bags, 26
bail, 26
baked, 76
balance, 26

balanced, 16, 26, 176
bald, 26
ball, 26, 51, 71, 77, 176, 178
ballistic, 26
balloon, 26
bananas, 72
band, 26
bandwagon, 36, 94
bang, 26, 71, 108
bank, 23, 26, 30, 40, 48, 88, 91, 109
bankable, 26
banker, 91
bankrolled, 26
bankrupt, 26
bankruptcy, 26
banned, 26
banner, 26
bar, 26, 138
barbecued, 26
bare, 26
barely, 26
Bargain, 46
bargain, 26, 71, 73, 128, 156, 164
bargained, 26
barn, 26
barred, 114
barrel, 51, 101
barrier, 26
barring, 26
barter, 26
base, 26, 30, 31, 42, 49, 96
Based, 46
based, 26, 80, 188
basement, 179
bases, 40
basic, 26
basically, 26
basics, 26

basket, 26
bastard, 26
bathrobe, 179
battered, 26
battery, 26
battle, 26
be, 4, 5, 20, 26, 27, 34, 46, 50, 85, 91, 112, 113, 153, 178, 179, 180, 184
beach, 27
beached, 27
beans, 176
bearable, 27
bearing, 34
beast, 27
beat, 27, 76, 118
beatable, 27
beaten, 27
beating, 27
beautiful, 27
beautifully, 27
beauty, 27, 35, 77, 155, 157
because, 27, 151
become, 27, 81
bedroom, 8, 179
beef, 27
been, 5, 21, 27, 58, 77, 84, 85, 91, 112, 162, 177
before, 27, 32, 113, 120, 125, 141, 169
beg, 27
begging, 27
begin, 27
beginner, 4, 27, 65
beginners, 65, 74
begins, 161
behavior, 32, 88
behind, 27, 84, 162
being, 27, 115, 140, 177, 178

belief, 27, 39
beliefs, 35
believability, 27
believable, 27, 41
believably, 27
believe, 27, 147, 184
believer, 64
believes, 3
believing, 104
belly, 27
belong, 27
belonging, 27
beloved, 177
below, 27, 138
belt, 71
bend, 27
beneath, 27
beneficial, 27, 63
beneficiary, 27
benefit, 27, 76, 84, 94, 119, 121
benefits, 18, 27, 39, 47, 54, 67, 84, 88, 106, 121, 125, 128, 141, 155, 160
bent, 27, 78
berry, 27
beside, 27
best, 28, 87, 90, 109, 113, 119, 161
bet, 85
beta, 28
better, 28, 32, 34, 63, 65, 92, 114, 151, 162, 184
between, 28, 50, 63, 87, 94, 138, 161
beware, 28
bewildering, 28
bewilderment, 28
bewitched, 28
beyond, 17, 28
bible, 28

bid, 120
Bidder, 46
bidding, 105
bids, 148
big, 23, 28, 86, 104, 156, 161, 162, 178, 179
bigger, 32
biggest, 28, 109, 161
bill, 36, 63, 176
billed, 28
billing, 28, 47
billion, 28
billionaire, 28
billions, 28
bills, 124, 125
binary, 28
bind, 28
binding, 28
bird, 54
birds, 96
birth, 28
birthday, 28
birthplace, 28
bit, 58
bite, 28
biting, 112
bitten, 76
bitter, 28
bitty, 92
biz, 64
bizarre, 28
black, 28, 87
blank, 63, 127, 180
blast, 28
blatant, 28
blazing, 29, 164
bleak, 29
blend, 168
blended, 29

bless, 29
blessed, 29
blessing, 29
blew, 29
blind, 29
blink, 118
blistering, 29, 76
blitz, 106
blizzard, 29
block, 4, 31
blockbuster, 29
blocked, 29
blonde, 29
blood, 29, 87, 113
blooded, 37, 67, 132
bloody, 29
blossom, 67
blossoming, 29
blow, 29
blowing, 107
blown, 29, 67, 76, 84
blows, 91
blue, 29, 119
blueprint, 16, 29
blueprints, 147
board, 29, 35
boatload, 148
bodacious, 29
bodied, 67
bodily, 29
body, 29
boggle, 29
boggling, 107
boil, 29
boiled, 29
boiling, 176
bold, 28, 29
boldly, 29
bolt, 29

bolts, 116, 161
bomb, 29, 163
bombard, 29
bona, 27, 29
bond, 142
bonded, 29
bonding, 29
bonds, 155
bone, 29
boned, 26
bonkers, 29
bonus, 18, 19, 29, 66, 71, 179
bonuses, 8, 10, 29, 71, 85, 96, 157, 184
Book, 1, 5
book, 3, 4, 5, 29, 32, 67, 119, 154
booked, 29
booklet, 66
books, 118
boom, 29
booming, 16, 29
boost, 29, 165
booster, 41
boosters, 130, 168
borderline, 29
born, 29, 112
boss, 27, 64, 96
both, 4, 72, 161
bottled, 29
bottom, 29, 67, 78, 114, 143
bottoming, 30
bottomless, 30
bottoms, 133
bought, 84, 125
bounce, 30
bounces, 176
bouncy, 30
bound, 30, 164
boundary, 30

bounds, 32, 99
box, 112, 141
boxed, 30
brace, 30
braced, 30
braided, 30
brain, 30, 184
brainer, 16, 114
brainy, 30
brand, 30, 48, 139
branded, 30
branding, 30, 109
brass, 30
brat, 30
bratty, 30
brave, 30
breach, 30
bread, 30, 113
break, 30, 62, 105, 113, 129, 136, 178
breakable, 30
breaking, 26, 30, 62, 74, 112, 139, 179
breakneck, 30
breakthrough, 28, 30, 51, 104, 126, 164
breath, 16
breathing, 64
breathtaking, 30
bred, 177
breeze, 16
breezy, 30
bribe, 30
bricks, 30, 100
brief, 16, 30
bright, 30
brightly, 30
brightness, 30
brilliant, 30

bring, 30
brink, 30
brisk, 30
brittle, 30
broad, 30
broadcast, 129
broadened, 30
broke, 30, 46, 72, 115
broken, 30
broker, 31, 108
bronze, 31
brought, 31
brown, 31
browse, 4, 31
brutally, 31
bubble, 31
buck, 108, 136
bucket, 16, 148
buckle, 31
buckled, 31
buddy, 31
budget, 21, 31, 47, 64, 65, 78, 88, 100, 102, 114, 118, 120, 149, 169, 188
budgeted, 31
buffed, 31
bug, 31
bugged, 31
build, 31, 81
building, 31, 160, 164, 176
built, 31, 42, 177
bulk, 31
bull, 31, 80
bullet, 31
bully, 31
bum, 31
bumpy, 31
bunched, 31
bundle, 104

charge, 35, 84, 86, 114, 140, 156, 185
charged, 56
charges, 115
charity, 35, 180
charmer, 35
charming, 35
chase, 43
chat, 35
chattering, 160
cheap, 16, 35, 49, 149
cheapskate, 35
cheat, 35
check, 28, 35, 37, 78, 108, 109, 113, 114, 176, 180
checked, 35, 84, 89, 130
checking, 161
checklist, 35
checkout, 35
checks, 28, 35, 94, 113, 141
cheerful, 35
chemical, 35
cherish, 35, 109
chest, 164
child, 16, 35
chill, 35
chilled, 35
chilling, 29
chilly, 35
chipped, 35
chips, 34
chock, 35
chocolate, 35
choice, 21, 47, 57, 59, 84, 101, 128, 136, 138, 148, 151, 156, 179
choices, 172
choose, 4, 35, 81, 126
choosing, 35
chopped, 35

chosen, 35, 46, 148, 177
chrome, 35
chronologically, 35
chunky, 35
cinch, 16
cinnamon, 35
circle, 36, 37, 67, 89
circular, 36
circulated, 36
circulation, 36, 113
circus, 36
citrus, 36
city, 36
claimed, 36
claims, 18, 149, 151
clarified, 36
class, 64, 102, 107, 130, 162, 170, 180
classed, 36
classic, 16, 36, 58, 163
classifiable, 36
classification, 36
classified, 36, 66
classy, 36
clean, 36, 153
cleanest, 36
cleaning, 147
cleansing, 36
clear, 36, 42, 66, 72, 102
cleared, 36
clearinghouse, 36
clearly, 36
clever, 36
cleverly, 36
click, 8, 36, 78, 79, 119, 124, 127
clicks, 63
client, 16, 31, 36, 101
clients, 16, 22, 79, 108, 120, 125, 131, 142

commission, 10, 37, 38, 100, 104, 118
commissioned, 38
commissions, 87
commitment, 28, 38, 64, 70, 74, 90, 100, 101, 104, 114, 125, 139, 148, 151
commitments, 155
committed, 38
commodity, 80
common, 38, 78, 92
commonsense, 38
commonwealth, 38
communication, 38, 39, 100, 140
communicator, 36
community, 38
commute, 114
compact, 38
companies, 28
companionable, 38
company, 18, 28, 38, 42, 47, 55, 64, 79, 88, 98, 104, 105, 128, 131, 149, 150, 156, 177
comparable, 38
comparative, 38
compare, 38
compared, 38
comparison, 124
compassionate, 38
compatibility, 38
compatible, 38
compelled, 38
compelling, 38
compensate, 38
compensated, 38
compensating, 38
compensation, 38, 101
compete, 38
competence, 50

competition, 27, 42, 47, 48, 49, 50, 54, 74, 80, 96, 100, 106, 118, 121, 132, 143, 148, 151, 154, 168
competitive, 38, 79
competitor, 38
competitors, 121
compilation, 46, 82, 172
compiled, 38
complaint, 109
complaints, 42
complete, 16, 38, 161, 162
completely, 27, 38, 85
completing, 38
complex, 38
complexed, 79
compliant, 38
complicated, 114
compliment, 125
complimentary, 38
compliments, 38
component, 57, 68, 88, 126, 173
composed, 38
comprehensive, 38, 161
compressed, 38
computable, 38
computed, 39
computer, 39, 105, 114, 179
computerize, 39
computerized, 39
concealed, 39
concept, 89, 113, 138, 168
concepts, 108
concerned, 99
concerns, 57
concise, 39
concluded, 105
conclusive, 39
concrete, 39
condensed, 39

cooked, 40
cool, 40
cooled, 19
cooler, 40
coolest, 40
cooperative, 40
coordinated, 40
cop, 50
copies, 92, 148, 177
copy, 16, 23, 40, 120, 141, 146
copyright, 40
Copywriter, 46
Copywriting, 4
copywriting, 3, 4
coral, 40
core, 40, 76
corners, 42, 112
corporate, 40, 163, 169
corporation, 28, 40, 156
corporations, 104, 109
correct, 40, 127
correcting, 148
corruptive, 40
cosmetic, 40
cosmic, 40
cost, 40, 42, 65, 102, 108, 114, 150, 172, 173, 180, 188
costly, 23, 40, 114
costs, 42, 43, 96, 102, 114, 115, 120, 121, 140, 143, 148, 150, 154
could, 16, 85, 91, 156, 177, 180
couldn, 40, 84
counseled, 40
countdown, 40, 161
counted, 40, 153
counter, 40, 80, 121
counteract, 40
counteractive, 40
counterblow, 40

counterclockwise, 40
countered, 40
counterpart, 40
counting, 40
countless, 40, 152
country, 40, 161
counts, 58
county, 40, 41
couple, 5, 16
coupon, 40, 108, 172
courageous, 40
course, 10, 40, 67
courteous, 40
courtesy, 40
cover, 40
coverage, 40, 67
covered, 35, 40, 91, 129, 172
covering, 40
covers, 40, 41
cow, 34
cowboy, 41
cozy, 41
crackdown, 41
cracking, 173
craft, 41
crafted, 64, 76, 136, 177
craftsmanship, 58, 64, 138, 140, 173
crafty, 41
crammed, 41
crank, 41
cranks, 41
cranny, 116
crash, 41
crave, 41
craving, 146
craze, 74, 98, 112
crazy, 41, 132, 148, 180, 184
cream, 41

cycle, 28, 43, 130
cycled, 43
cycloned, 43
daily, 46, 56, 57
dainty, 46
dairy, 46
damage, 114
damp, 46
dandy, 64
danger, 46
dangerous, 46
dangerously, 100
dangling, 46
dare, 46
daring, 46
dark, 46
darken, 46
darling, 46
darn, 46
data, 46, 169
database, 46
date, 16, 28, 46, 120, 132, 141, 169
dated, 113, 115
dates, 139
day, 10, 14, 16, 19, 46, 51, 73, 74,
87, 91, 94, 105, 108, 110, 119, 120,
136, 146, 147
daydream, 46
days, 10, 14, 18, 84, 149
dazzle, 138
dazzling, 46
dead, 46, 51
deadbeat, 46
deadline, 46, 48, 155, 163
deadlines, 107
deadlocked, 46
deal, 22, 26, 28, 36, 46, 73, 113,
119, 124, 141, 155, 157, 162, 177,
178, 179

dealer, 178
Dealers, 46
deals, 36, 41
Dear, 46
dearly, 46
death, 100, 156
debated, 46
debit, 46
debt, 26, 46, 47, 55, 71
debugged, 47
debut, 47
decade, 47
decades, 86
decaffeinated, 47
decay, 47
deceased, 47
deceived, 47
decent, 47
decently, 47
deceptive, 47
decide, 47, 81, 163
decided, 47
deciding, 47
decipher, 47
decision, 41, 47, 150
decisional, 47
decisions, 126
decisive, 47
deck, 153
decline, 136
decode, 47
deconstructed, 47
decorated, 47
decreased, 47
dedicate, 47
dedicated, 3, 47
Dedication, 1, 3
deducted, 47
deductible, 47, 160

designated, 48
designed, 16, 36, 42, 48, 90, 130, 152, 176
desirable, 48
desire, 31, 150
desired, 48
desires, 39
desk, 78
desperate, 48
destination, 59
destiny, 16, 35, 48, 106
destroy, 48
destructible, 48
destruction, 48
destructive, 48
detachable, 48
detail, 41, 48, 67, 125, 128, 142, 173
detailed, 16, 48, 60, 143
detailing, 48
details, 90, 142
detected, 48
detective, 48
determination, 48
determine, 48, 81
determined, 30, 48
detrimental, 48
develop, 48, 81
developed, 48, 92
developer, 48
developing, 48
development, 130, 141, 148
developments, 59, 90
device, 108, 163
devilish, 48
devise, 36
devoted, 48
diabolic, 48
diagnosed, 49

diagonal, 49
diagrammed, 49
dial, 49
diamond, 16, 49
did, 49
didn, 49
die, 49, 163
diet, 49
dietary, 49
difference, 91, 149, 155, 161
different, 10, 46, 49
difficult, 49
digest, 49
digger, 73
digit, 51
digital, 49
digitally, 34
dignified, 49
diligent, 49
dim, 49
dime, 16
dimension, 113, 162
dimensional, 49, 119, 163
diminish, 49
dingy, 49
dink, 143
dinosaur, 49
dip, 49
diploma, 49
diplomatic, 49
dire, 49
direct, 49, 71
directed, 49
directional, 49
directions, 65, 154
directors, 29
dirt, 16, 49
dirty, 49, 51
disability, 49

dolled, 71
domain, 50
domestic, 50
dominate, 50
don, 50, 51, 84, 184
donation, 50
done, 146
dooms, 51
door, 37, 71
doors, 27
doorway, 51
dormant, 51
dory, 82
dotcom, 51, 153
dots, 39
double, 51, 81
doubled, 51
doubtful, 51
dough, 138
down, 21, 30, 31, 37, 42, 51, 70, 72, 76, 96, 99, 105, 112, 114, 116, 126, 128, 133, 146, 162, 176, 180
downgraded, 51
downhill, 51
downline, 51
download, 34, 51, 67, 115
downloadable, 51, 86
downs, 170
downside, 51
downsizing, 51
downtrend, 51
downturn, 105
dozen, 16
dozens, 51, 71
drafted, 51
drafty, 51
drag, 51
drain, 128
drama, 51

dramatic, 51
dramatically, 51
draped, 51
drastic, 51
draw, 51
drawback, 51
drawing, 51
drawn, 51
dream, 51, 56, 67, 101, 160, 161, 162, 165
dreams, 28, 63, 65, 138, 139
drench, 51
dressed, 51, 177
dried, 42, 51
drive, 38, 76, 161
driven, 22, 27, 36, 40, 42, 48, 51, 55, 59, 62, 63, 67, 72, 80, 84, 85, 86, 91, 94, 101, 105, 109, 128, 130, 136, 146, 164, 172
driving, 51
droopy, 51
drop, 16, 51
dropping, 94
drought, 51
drug, 21, 51
drum, 52
dry, 29, 42, 52, 67
due, 52, 101, 125
duplicable, 52
duplicate, 52
duplicating, 148
duplication, 52
durable, 52
during, 132
duty, 52, 77, 100, 118, 184
dwarfs, 52
dyed, 52
dyer, 52
dynamic, 52

eligibility, 55
eligible, 55
eliminate, 55, 81
eliminated, 55
eliminating, 46, 55
elite, 55
else, 77, 85, 162
elude, 55
elusive, 55
elusiveness, 55
email, 20, 55, 66
embark, 55
embarrass, 55
embedded, 55
embrace, 55
embracing, 19
emerald, 55
emerge, 55
emergence, 55
emergency, 55
emerging, 55
emotion, 55, 85
emotional, 18, 55, 56
emotionally, 56
empathy, 56
emphasize, 56
empire, 28, 31, 56, 130, 153
employ, 56
employable, 56
employed, 4, 56, 89, 148
employee, 56, 114
employees, 51, 63, 109, 114, 142
employer, 56
empty, 50, 56
emulate, 56
enable, 56
enabled, 56
enchanting, 56
enchantment, 56

enclosed, 56
encoded, 56
encounter, 56
encourage, 56
encouraged, 56
encrypted, 56
encryption, 56
encyclopedia, 56
end, 26, 38, 46, 56, 78, 106, 184
endangered, 56
endeavor, 56
endeavors, 4
ended, 119
ending, 17, 112
endless, 56, 115, 128
endorse, 84, 169
endorsed, 56, 79
endorsements, 56, 138
ends, 56, 118
enduring, 56
energetic, 56
energize, 56
energy, 56, 60, 78, 163, 168
enforced, 56
engaged, 56
engineered, 56
English, 180
engraved, 56
engross, 56
engulfed, 56
enhance, 56
enhanced, 56
enhances, 56
enhancing, 56, 87, 136, 142, 153
enjoy, 56
enjoyable, 56
enjoyed, 56
enjoyment, 56
enlarge, 56

enlarged, 56
enlighten, 56
enlightened, 56
enlightening, 56
enlist, 56
enlisted, 57
enormous, 54, 57, 70
enough, 28, 150
enraged, 57
enriched, 57
enriching, 57
enroll, 57
ensure, 57, 81
entangle, 57
entangled, 57
enter, 57
entering, 57
enterprise, 57, 66, 79, 94
enterprising, 57
entertain, 57
entertained, 57
entertainer, 57
entertaining, 57
entertainment, 57
enthusiasm, 57, 168
Enthusiast, 46
enthusiastic, 57
enthusiasts, 102
entice, 57
enticing, 57
entire, 57
entirely, 57
entrancing, 57
Entrepreneur, 46
entrepreneur, 57, 58, 184
entrepreneurs, 57
entrust, 57
entry, 57
envelope, 133

envious, 57
environment, 57
environmental, 57
environmentally, 57
envision, 57
envy, 57
epic, 57
epidemic, 57
equal, 57, 148
equipment, 18, 31, 39, 57, 98, 108, 114, 140, 141, 152
equipped, 57
equity, 57
era, 57
erasable, 57
erased, 57
erotic, 57
erotica, 57
errand, 57
error, 57, 164
errorless, 57
erupt, 57
escape, 57
escaping, 57
escorted, 57
especially, 4
essence, 57, 163
essential, 57
establish, 57, 58, 81
established, 58, 73, 101, 177
estimated, 58
etc, 18
eternal, 3, 58
eternity, 58
ethical, 58, 78, 184
ethically, 58, 99
ethics, 58, 106
etiquette, 106
evaluated, 58

evaporated, 58

even, 4, 30, 50, 58

evening, 73

event, 46, 58, 109, 113, 126, 153

eventually, 58

ever, 28, 50, 58, 77, 79, 85, 98, 108, 150, 180

everlasting, 58

every, 5, 8, 10, 14, 28, 36, 40, 41, 54, 58, 71, 78, 85, 86, 96, 113, 124, 128, 140, 155, 161, 177, 180

everyday, 99, 115, 131, 180

everyone, 20, 58, 92, 116

everything, 17, 23, 40, 41, 58, 71, 99, 108, 161, 163

everywhere, 91, 184

evidence, 36, 38, 39, 58, 88, 155, 168

exact, 58, 161

exactly, 58, 81, 85, 99

examination, 58, 143

examine, 99

examined, 58

example, 58, 65

examples, 10, 36, 58, 116, 139, 152, 172

exceed, 58

exceeded, 91

exceeding, 58

excellence, 58

excellent, 58, 77, 87

except, 58

exceptional, 58

exceptionally, 58

exceptions, 109

excerpt, 66

excess, 59

excessively, 59

exchange, 42, 59

excited, 84

exciting, 59

exclude, 59

exclusive, 59

exclusivity, 59

excuse, 59

execute, 59

executed, 59

Executive, 46

executive, 59

executives, 163

exempt, 59, 160

exempted, 59

exemption, 59

exercise, 59

exercised, 59

exhausted, 59

exhaustive, 5

exhibited, 59

exhilarated, 59

exhilarating, 59

existing, 59

exists, 138

exotic, 59

expand, 59

expandability, 59

expandable, 59

expanded, 16, 59

expanding, 59, 80, 107, 153

expands, 59

expansion, 59, 119, 154

expect, 59

expectations, 28, 58, 78, 139

expected, 62, 108

expedited, 59

expendable, 59

expenditures, 59

expense, 59, 115, 152

expenses, 115, 120, 172

expensive, 59, 99, 114, 120
experience, 30, 50, 59, 60, 64, 70, 76, 84, 85, 90, 99, 114, 115, 139, 140, 142, 143, 148, 164, 168, 184
experienced, 59
experiences, 26, 58
experiential, 59
experiment, 59
experimentation, 59
experimented, 59
expert, 17, 26, 27, 59, 65, 71, 116, 121, 139, 140, 152, 178, 184
expertise, 59, 78
experts, 59, 88, 124, 127, 160, 164, 177, 180
explain, 150
explained, 36, 60
explanation, 60
explicit, 60
explode, 60
exploded, 60
exploit, 60
explore, 60
explosion, 60
explosive, 60
exported, 60
exposed, 58, 60
exposure, 60, 66, 160
express, 60
expressed, 60
expressible, 60
exquisite, 60
exquisitely, 60
extend, 60
extended, 60
extensible, 60
extensive, 60
exterminate, 60
external, 60

extinct, 60
extinction, 60
extinguished, 60
extra, 20, 60, 63, 104, 114, 138, 163, 177
extracted, 60
extraction, 60
extraordinary, 60
extrasensory, 60
extravagant, 60
extravaganza, 178
extreme, 60
extremely, 60
eye, 30, 31, 60, 80, 119, 147
eyeballs, 96
eyebrow, 60
eyebrows, 138
eyed, 36, 153
eyewitness, 60
eyewitnesses, 60
ezine, 60, 66
fabricated, 62
fabulous, 62
face, 62, 114
faced, 67, 127, 148
faceless, 62
faceted, 109
facets, 59
facility, 58, 94, 152, 154
fact, 17, 62, 78, 91, 96, 106, 132, 147, 161, 162
factor, 41, 47, 62, 86
factoring, 62
factors, 54
factory, 62
facts, 37, 50, 62, 64, 71, 76, 91, 138, 140, 160, 162, 164
factual, 62
faculty, 180

fad, 62, 98, 113
fail, 62, 86, 109, 161, 178, 184
failing, 113, 179
failure, 28, 62
faint, 62
fair, 62
faith, 62, 73
faithfully, 62
fake, 62
fall, 50, 62, 143
fallen, 62
fame, 62
familiar, 62, 84
familiarized, 62
family, 62
famine, 62, 63
famous, 27, 62, 180
fan, 23, 62
fancy, 62
fans, 41, 138
fantasies, 62
fantasize, 62
fantastic, 104
fantasy, 67
FAQ, 138
far, 62, 63, 91
fascinating, 62
fashion, 62, 118
fashionable, 62
fashioned, 62
fast, 22, 48, 62, 63, 77, 100, 125, 148
faster, 36, 63, 77, 168
fastest, 63, 161
fat, 63, 102
fatal, 63
fate, 63
father, 63
fault, 114

favor, 50, 163
favorable, 63
favored, 177
favorite, 63, 80
fear, 63
feared, 63
fearless, 63
feasible, 63
feast, 63
featured, 63
features, 16, 18, 20, 63, 78, 90, 155
fed, 153
federal, 63
fee, 18, 63, 64, 115, 119
feed, 63
feedback, 63
feeding, 114
feel, 16, 49, 63, 82, 184
feeling, 76, 82, 85, 94, 136, 151
fees, 94, 114, 115, 179
feet, 10, 71
Fellow, 46
felt, 12, 63, 77
female, 19
festival, 63
festive, 63
fetched, 62
few, 16, 63, 65, 86, 94, 121, 162, 179
fewer, 63
fiber, 63
fictional, 63
fide, 27, 29
field, 27, 59, 63, 65, 119, 132
fielded, 63
fighting, 114
figure, 10, 14, 26, 63, 149, 150, 153, 177, 179
figured, 63

founders, 66
four, 66
fourth, 66
foxy, 66
fraction, 66
fragile, 66
fragrance, 21, 56, 66
framed, 66
framework, 66
franchise, 116
franchised, 66
franchising, 66
fraud, 66
freak, 66
freaky, 66
free, 8, 10, 14, 16, 18, 19, 20, 21, 30, 34, 35, 37, 38, 40, 42, 47, 49, 51, 52, 55, 57, 59, 63, 66, 67, 70, 71, 76, 77, 89, 90, 94, 96, 104, 116, 120, 124, 125, 127, 128, 129, 130, 140, 141, 142, 143, 149, 151, 152, 155, 160, 162, 163, 164, 179, 180
freebie, 67
freebies, 10
freedom, 63, 67, 70, 71, 139, 164, 176
freelanced, 67
freelancing, 67
freely, 67
freeze, 67
frenzy, 41, 67
frequency, 67, 78
frequent, 67
fresh, 16, 67, 99
fresher, 67
freshly, 67
friction, 67
fried, 67
Friend, 46

friend, 16, 67, 138
friendly, 21, 30, 31, 37, 42, 47, 49, 50, 56, 57, 60, 62, 63, 67, 70, 85, 96, 107, 112, 113, 116, 120, 124, 125, 126, 129, 130, 131, 136, 138, 140, 141, 142, 143, 155, 156, 170, 172, 173
friends, 10, 91
frighten, 67
frigid, 67
fringe, 67
frisky, 67
from, 4, 8, 16, 17, 18, 20, 21, 30, 31, 32, 37, 47, 55, 57, 58, 59, 60, 63, 64, 67, 72, 73, 84, 85, 91, 99, 108, 112, 119, 125, 127, 130, 138, 143, 146, 147, 148, 153, 179, 180
front, 67
fronted, 67
frost, 67
frosted, 67
frown, 67
frozen, 67
frugal, 67
fruity, 67
frustration, 71, 179
fuel, 67
fugitive, 67
fulfill, 67
fulfilled, 67
fulfilling, 67, 77
fulfillment, 23, 67, 114
full, 10, 16, 26, 35, 37, 41, 67, 68, 87, 124, 138, 160
fullest, 163
fully, 68
fun, 68
function, 42, 68, 128, 173
functional, 68

handwritten, 179
handy, 76
hang, 76
hanging, 163
happen, 104
happiness, 59
happy, 76, 96
hard, 23, 37, 49, 60, 76, 114, 143, 148, 179
hardball, 76, 127
hardened, 26
harder, 101, 179, 180
hardship, 76
hardware, 77
hardworking, 77
harm, 29
harmful, 77
harmless, 77
harness, 77, 99
harsh, 77
harshly, 77
harvest, 77
has, 5, 12, 20, 21, 77, 91, 162
hassle, 77, 179
hassles, 107
hat, 76
hatched, 31
haul, 101
haunted, 77
haunting, 77
have, 3, 4, 12, 28, 50, 58, 77, 81, 84, 85, 92, 99, 100, 105, 109, 113, 125, 151, 162, 164, 176, 177, 184
haven, 77
having, 4, 57, 77, 141
hazardous, 77
he, 3
head, 37, 77
headache, 77

headaches, 115
headed, 31, 36, 51
header, 51
headline, 77, 154
heads, 77
headway, 77
healing, 77
health, 73
healthy, 77
heard, 12, 20, 22, 58, 77, 84, 85, 113, 147, 176, 184, 185
heart, 54, 65, 77
hearted, 28, 37, 67, 76, 176
heartfelt, 77
hearty, 77
heat, 77, 147
heated, 77
heating, 19
heaven, 77
heavenly, 77
heavier, 77
heavily, 77
heavy, 77
heels, 77
hefty, 77, 78
heighten, 78
heights, 152
held, 55, 76, 129, 132
hell, 65, 78
hello, 78
help, 4, 5, 31, 35, 48, 57, 66, 78, 85, 91, 106, 129, 154, 160, 163, 164, 173
helped, 78
helpful, 10, 78
helping, 88
helpless, 78
helps, 58, 78
here, 36, 57, 78, 91, 161, 179, 184

inspiring, 23
install, 54, 81, 188
installation, 89
installed, 89, 130
installment, 89
instant, 17, 20, 70, 89, 119, 184
instantaneous, 89
instantly, 34, 73, 81, 89, 149, 160, 172
instincts, 65
instituted, 89
institution, 89, 130, 177
instructed, 90
instruction, 48, 107
instructional, 90
instructions, 38, 58, 90, 149, 154
instrumental, 90
insubstantial, 90
insufficient, 90
insulated, 90
insurable, 90
insurance, 18, 60, 90
insure, 90
insured, 68, 90
intacted, 90
intangible, 90
integral, 90
integrate, 90
integrated, 90
integrity, 64, 90
intellect, 90
intellectual, 90
intellectually, 90
intelligence, 67, 90, 148, 168
intelligent, 27, 90, 184
intense, 72, 90
intensifiers, 146
intensify, 90
intensity, 78

intensive, 90
intent, 90
interaction, 39
interactive, 90
interchangeable, 90
interest, 41, 51, 72, 84, 90, 102, 114, 129, 155
interested, 34, 71, 96
interesting, 90
interests, 87
interfaced, 90
interior, 90
interlocking, 90
intermediate, 90
internal, 90
internally, 90
international, 90
internationally, 90
Internet, 20, 66, 90, 102, 114, 160
interpreted, 90
interrupt, 90
intervention, 90
interview, 90
interviewed, 90
intimate, 90
into, 34, 40, 42, 49, 71, 81, 127, 150, 157, 160, 164, 165
intoxicating, 90
intriguing, 90
introduce, 99
introducing, 90
introduction, 90
introductory, 90
intruder, 91
intuition, 91
intuitive, 91
invalid, 91
invaluable, 91
invent, 91

joining, 58
joint, 94
jointure, 99
joy, 129
joyful, 94
judged, 85, 94
judgment, 73, 94
judgmental, 94
judicial, 94
juices, 4
juicy, 94
jump, 94
junky, 94
just, 26, 84, 91, 92, 94, 108, 125, 140, 156, 161, 162, 184
justice, 94
justifiable, 94
justified, 94
karat, 10
keen, 96
keep, 85, 96, 120
keeps, 96, 127
kept, 27, 28, 177
key, 10, 78, 96, 101, 102, 118, 161
keyed, 102
keynote, 96
keys, 162
kick, 96
kicking, 19, 32, 99
kid, 96
kidding, 85
kill, 96
killer, 96, 124
killing, 104
kind, 64, 96, 119
kindhearted, 96
kinds, 10
king, 64, 96
kiss, 96

kissable, 96
kit, 153
kitchen, 179
knee, 96
knit, 36
knock, 96
know, 20, 49, 50, 51, 58, 81, 84, 85, 96, 109, 169, 177, 184
knowing, 82, 161
knowledge, 10, 38, 57, 59, 70, 89, 92, 96, 114, 115, 128, 129, 162, 172
knowledgeable, 96
known, 90, 96, 99, 100, 147, 161, 177
Kowalenko, 4
lab, 98
labor, 98
laboring, 98
laced, 98
lackluster, 98
ladder, 169
laden, 130
ladylike, 98
lagged, 94
laid, 98, 112
lame, 98
land, 98
landmark, 98
language, 36, 180
lap, 87
large, 4, 98, 114
larger, 98
largest, 98, 180
laser, 98
lasering, 98
last, 71, 94, 98
lasting, 41, 58, 98, 101
latch, 98

man, 81, 105, 143
manage, 81, 105, 114
manageable, 105
managed, 28, 105, 150
management, 105, 108, 136, 152
mandatory, 105
maneuver, 105, 154
maneuverability, 105
maneuvers, 150
manhandled, 105
manifest, 105
manipulated, 105
manipulation, 105
mankind, 105
mannered, 85
mans, 98
manual, 105
manufactured, 105
many, 5, 22, 35, 36, 59, 60, 63, 78, 81, 102, 105, 126, 128, 130, 131, 139, 142, 148
map, 105, 143, 164
maple, 105
margin, 78, 79, 130
marginal, 105
margins, 79
markdown, 105
marked, 105, 177
market, 18, 27, 28, 40, 48, 55, 62, 63, 66, 72, 98, 105, 113, 120, 147, 148, 149, 151, 160, 163, 169, 176, 178
marketability, 105
marketed, 106
Marketer, 46
marketer, 72, 184
marketers, 59, 79

marketing, 23, 49, 54, 55, 60, 72, 90, 96, 106, 112, 113, 119, 132, 150, 161, 163, 164, 173, 176
markets, 113, 160
markup, 106
maroon, 106
marquee, 106
marriage, 106
marvelous, 106
masculine, 106
mashed, 106
masked, 106
mass, 41, 106
massive, 16, 106
master, 106, 161, 176
mastermind, 106
masterpiece, 99, 106, 129, 154, 163
masters, 106
match, 34, 125
matched, 91, 106
matchless, 106
material, 41, 55, 62, 80, 88, 106, 140, 146, 147
materials, 54, 64, 136, 155
maternal, 106
mathematical, 106
matrix, 65
matter, 91, 106, 114
mature, 106
mauve, 106
max, 163
maximize, 106
maximized, 106
maximum, 71, 104, 106
may, 5, 58, 184
maybe, 106
MB, 121

mind, 35, 91, 105, 107, 126, 131, 178, 179
minded, 17, 30, 98, 100, 112, 120, 148, 150, 155
mindful, 107
minds, 125
mindset, 176
mine, 10, 16, 73, 78
mingled, 107
mini, 107
miniature, 107
minimal, 107
minimize, 107
minimized, 107
minimum, 104, 108, 114, 131
minor, 108
minority, 108
mint, 108, 120
minute, 16, 58, 98, 109, 169, 170
minutes, 17, 27, 51, 71, 77, 85, 86, 87, 94, 131, 160, 179
miracle, 22, 23, 108, 156
miraculous, 108
misinformation, 114
miss, 51, 80, 112
mission, 108, 152, 173
mistake, 51, 108, 161
mistaken, 108
mistakes, 10, 23, 49, 99, 108, 146, 161
mix, 62, 106, 130
mixable, 108
mixed, 108
mixture, 108, 147, 160
mlm, 108
mobile, 108
modal, 50
model, 31, 80, 130
modeled, 108

models, 132
moderate, 108
moderated, 108
modern, 108
modernized, 108
modest, 108
modifiable, 108
modified, 108
modifiers, 146
moist, 108
mom, 108
moment, 41, 47, 90, 108, 138, 147, 168
momentum, 104
money, 28, 41, 51, 54, 56, 60, 65, 71, 73, 76, 77, 82, 85, 88, 89, 100, 104, 105, 106, 108, 113, 114, 115, 118, 128, 133, 146, 148, 150, 152, 153, 160, 163, 172, 179, 185
moneymaker, 108
monitored, 108
monitors, 37
monopoly, 108
monster, 108
month, 8, 10, 65, 86, 104, 119, 121, 131, 142
monthly, 41, 108, 115, 125
months, 10, 29, 84, 109, 149
monumental, 108
moon, 119, 131
moral, 184
morale, 108
more, 3, 8, 40, 54, 62, 70, 71, 72, 92, 105, 108, 112, 115, 132, 142, 148, 168, 176
morning, 114
mortal, 108
mortar, 30
mortgage, 108

most, 38, 49, 65, 71, 85, 91, 108, 109, 119, 161, 162, 177, 178
mother, 109
motherly, 109
motivate, 109
motivated, 79, 109
motivation, 109
motivational, 109
motive, 99, 109, 130
mountain, 109
mouse, 35, 63
mouth, 109, 133, 179
movable, 109
move, 105
movers, 109
moves, 105
moving, 63, 150, 157
much, 104, 109, 114
multi, 109
multibrand, 109
multifunctional, 109
multilevel, 109
multimedia, 109
multiple, 109, 125, 148
multiplied, 109
multiply, 109
multiplying, 176
multitude, 4
municipal, 109
mushroomed, 109
musical, 109
must, 10, 16, 109, 178
muted, 109
mutual, 109
mutually, 109
my, 8, 16, 26, 35, 40, 51, 52, 78, 85, 87, 91, 99, 109, 110, 121, 152, 184
myself, 99

mysterious, 110
mystery, 110
mystic, 110
mystical, 110
myth, 21, 110, 127
mythical, 110
myths, 162
nail, 112
nailed, 112
naked, 112
Name, 1, 11
name, 12, 28, 30, 31, 46, 109, 119, 124, 132
named, 112
nameless, 112
names, 161
narrow, 112
nasty, 112
nation, 112, 161
national, 109, 112
nationally, 112
nationwide, 112
natural, 19, 112
naturally, 112
nature, 85, 112
naughty, 112
navigated, 112
navigation, 112
near, 112
neat, 112
neato, 112
necessary, 112
necessity, 17, 112
neck, 112
necked, 154
need, 20, 49, 51, 52, 58, 71, 87, 92, 112, 161, 177, 178, 184
needed, 41, 114, 115
NeedHim, 3

needles, 126
needs, 31, 112
needy, 112
negative, 112
negotiable, 112
negotiate, 112
negotiated, 112
neighborly, 112
neon, 112
nerve, 71, 112
nest, 112
net, 112
netiquette, 112
netted, 112
network, 31, 41, 112
networked, 112
networking, 112
never, 28, 81, 112, 113, 116, 162, 178, 184
new, 4, 16, 20, 22, 30, 32, 42, 48, 49, 57, 60, 70, 72, 99, 100, 113, 127, 128, 138, 152, 165, 178
newbie, 113
newbies, 113
newer, 113
newest, 113
newfound, 113
newly, 113
news, 30, 59, 62, 113, 140, 148, 163
newscast, 113
newsletter, 19, 66
newsworthiness, 113
newsworthy, 113
next, 65, 87, 113, 120, 161
nice, 113
niche, 34, 105, 113
nick, 87
nifty, 113

night, 19, 65, 73, 105, 113, 114, 116
nightly, 113
nights, 115
nimble, 113
nine, 113
nippy, 114
nitty, 114
NIV, 3
No, 182
no, 5, 10, 16, 22, 35, 50, 54, 58, 59, 62, 65, 71, 78, 84, 85, 86, 87, 91, 92, 94, 96, 99, 100, 104, 108, 109, 114, 115, 116, 119, 121, 126, 128, 131, 138, 140, 141, 148, 149, 150, 152, 153, 160, 161, 162, 163, 172, 173, 177, 178, 179, 184, 185
noble, 115
noise, 115
non, 16
nonabrasive, 115
nonacid, 115
nonaddicting, 115
nonaddictive, 115
nonadditive, 115
noncompetitive, 115
nonconforming, 115
nondisclosure, 115
none, 147
noneffective, 115
nonessential, 115
nonexplosive, 115
nonfiction, 115
nonfictional, 115
nonflammable, 115
nongovernment, 116
nonhuman, 116
nonindustrial, 116
nonlethal, 116

outrage, 121
outrageous, 121, 179
outrageously, 121
outright, 121
outs, 20, 89
outscore, 121
outsell, 121
outshine, 121
outside, 121
outsmart, 121
outsourcing, 121
outspend, 121
outspoken, 121
outstanding, 121
over, 27, 29, 31, 32, 48, 54, 64, 72, 77, 84, 91, 92, 101, 105, 112, 118, 121, 125, 138, 146, 149, 152, 165, 178, 179, 180
overactive, 121
overall, 109, 121
overcome, 81, 121
overcrowded, 121
overdrive, 121
overemphasis, 121
overexcited, 121
overexposure, 121
overflowing, 121
overhaul, 121
overhauled, 121
overhead, 102, 114, 115, 121
overindulge, 121
overjoyed, 121
overlooked, 109, 121
overnight, 71, 87, 104, 121
overpowering, 121
overrides, 121
overriding, 121
oversized, 121
oversold, 121

overstate, 121
overstocked, 121
oversupply, 121
overtake, 121
overwhelmed, 121
overwhelming, 121, 122
overworked, 122
owe, 122, 184
own, 18, 27, 34, 35, 41, 42, 106, 116, 119, 120, 122, 153, 180, 184
owned, 35, 108, 122, 125, 128
Owner, 46
owner, 31, 119, 122
owning, 161
pace, 63
pacesetter, 124
pack, 19
package, 16, 38, 98, 124, 130, 141, 143, 150, 154
packaged, 124
packaging, 50, 86, 115, 124
packed, 10, 94, 124, 128, 139, 172
packs, 124
padded, 124
padding, 124
page, 5, 67, 71, 119, 120, 176
pages, 10, 121
paid, 27, 71, 79, 84, 124, 125, 177
pain, 23, 115, 124
painful, 124
painstaking, 124
paint, 124
painted, 76, 124
paired, 124
pajamas, 179
palace, 124
pales, 124
palm, 124
pamper, 124

product, 10, 12, 23, 38, 41, 42, 59, 80, 84, 87, 89, 91, 115, 119, 130, 131, 146, 156, 169, 179, 184

production, 120, 130

productive, 40, 79, 130

productivity, 130

products, 18, 20, 41, 48, 78, 79, 84, 100, 102, 109, 119, 143, 147, 148, 153, 178, 179

profession, 130

professional, 16, 130

professionally, 130

professionals, 88, 139

proficiency, 130

proficient, 130, 172

profile, 42, 79, 102, 130

profiled, 130

profit, 23, 72, 76, 79, 94, 121, 130, 132, 141, 148, 156, 169

profitability, 130

profitable, 27, 31, 41, 89, 130, 131, 156, 178

profiting, 27

profits, 26, 29, 58, 60, 63, 78, 85, 87, 88, 96, 106, 112, 118, 119, 121, 131, 136, 138, 143, 150, 153, 155, 157, 164, 168

profound, 4, 131

program, 19, 22, 31, 37, 94, 107, 131, 141

programmable, 131

programmed, 131

programmer, 131

programming, 115, 131

progressive, 131

prohibited, 131

project, 38, 131

projectable, 131

projected, 131

projects, 131

prolific, 131

prolong, 131

prominent, 131

promise, 28, 48, 84, 85, 126, 131, 140

promises, 131

promising, 131

promo, 131

promote, 81, 131, 156

promoted, 131

promoting, 131

promotion, 41, 42, 70, 107, 114, 131, 146

promotional, 28, 39, 125, 131

prompt, 131

prompted, 131

promptly, 131

prone, 17, 19, 88, 131

proof, 17, 19, 21, 22, 26, 27, 30, 31, 35, 36, 37, 38, 39, 40, 41, 42, 47, 49, 50, 52, 56, 57, 60, 62, 63, 64, 65, 66, 67, 68, 70, 72, 73, 76, 77, 78, 82, 84, 85, 87, 88, 91, 99, 101, 105, 108, 115, 120, 127, 128, 130, 131, 132, 136, 139, 143, 146, 151, 152, 155, 157, 160, 162, 169, 172, 173, 176

proofread, 131

propaganda, 131

propel, 131

proper, 131

properly, 4

property, 90

prophet, 131

proportional, 131

proportions, 22, 57, 82

proposal, 17, 36, 131

proposition, 14

quenching, 136, 162
quest, 136
question, 22, 31, 99, 136, 162
questionable, 136
questions, 10, 21, 42, 115
quick, 4, 16, 71, 78, 136
quickest, 136
quickly, 5, 81, 142, 156
quiet, 96, 136
quilted, 136
quit, 136
quite, 92, 136, 162
quiz, 136
quota, 136, 146
quotable, 136
quoted, 136
race, 99, 138
racked, 138
racking, 112
radar, 138
radiant, 138
radical, 138
radio, 138
rags, 67, 138
rain, 138
raise, 72, 138
raised, 29, 138
raiser, 68
raising, 21, 60, 76, 138, 148, 179
rake, 138
Randall, 4
random, 138
randomly, 138
range, 101, 129, 149, 178
ranging, 178
ranked, 138
ranking, 71, 79
rankings, 17, 71
rant, 138

rap, 31
rapid, 138
rapport, 58, 104
rare, 119, 138
rarely, 84, 138
rarest, 138
rat, 99, 138
rate, 42, 43, 49, 64, 78, 84, 90, 102, 138, 142, 147, 162
rated, 79, 138, 164
rates, 4, 29, 51, 79, 102, 139, 140
rating, 21, 64, 109
ratio, 40, 78, 88, 146, 173
rational, 138
rave, 138
raving, 41, 138
ravish, 138
raw, 138
razor, 138
razzle, 138
re, 84, 85, 87, 114, 125, 178, 184, 185
reaccept, 138
reach, 138
reachable, 138
reaching, 62
reaction, 18, 109, 138
reactions, 138
reactive, 138
read, 16, 54, 84, 85, 109, 138, 139
readable, 139
reader, 139
readers, 71, 139
readership, 88
ready, 21, 34, 41, 43, 73, 85, 120, 139
reaffirm, 139
real, 101, 139, 162
realign, 139

reproduction, 115, 141
reprogram, 141
reps, 146
reputable, 141
reputation, 64, 86, 90, 98, 109, 141, 151, 168, 169, 180, 184
request, 141
requested, 141
require, 23
required, 21, 114, 115, 124, 141, 142
requirement, 112
requirements, 141, 146
requires, 141
resale, 141
research, 5, 48, 91, 105, 141, 146, 151, 163, 184
researched, 141, 162
researching, 152
resell, 14, 66, 100, 141
Reseller, 46
reseller, 37, 94, 141
resemblance, 60
reserve, 114, 141, 176
reserves, 115
reshape, 141
residence, 141
residential, 141
residual, 28, 41, 101, 141
resist, 76, 115, 132
resistance, 100, 107, 141, 173
resistant, 107, 139, 144, 149
resolvable, 141
resort, 98
resource, 4, 119, 141
resourceful, 141
resources, 10, 19, 87, 99, 169, 172
respectable, 141
respected, 79, 142

respond, 142
responds, 142
response, 29, 49, 51, 56, 70, 79, 131, 136, 139, 142
responses, 136
responsibility, 142
responsible, 142
responsive, 142
rest, 16
restock, 142
restored, 68, 142
restriction, 142
restrictive, 142
restructure, 142
restructured, 142
restyled, 142
result, 5, 142
resulted, 142
results, 20, 34, 35, 48, 59, 62, 63, 71, 74, 79, 88, 89, 90, 100, 106, 109, 127, 130, 136, 151, 157, 163
resurging, 142
retail, 142
retain, 142
retention, 86
retire, 125, 142
retired, 142
retirement, 54, 142, 180
retiring, 142
retroactive, 142
retrospective, 142
return, 71, 79, 105, 136, 138, 142
returnable, 142
returns, 77, 107, 140, 142
revamp, 142
revamped, 142
reveal, 85
revealed, 142, 147
revealing, 142

rub, 143
rubber, 31
rugged, 143
ruining, 143
rule, 143
rules, 10, 27, 143
run, 23, 62, 87, 143, 149, 153, 162
runned, 19, 50, 105
running, 118, 143, 163
rural, 144
rush, 18, 73, 144
rust, 144
rusty, 144
saddle, 26
safe, 36, 57, 62, 107, 127, 146, 161, 162
safeguarded, 146
safety, 146
said, 12, 146, 153, 177
salary, 146
sale, 8, 14, 21, 36, 96, 118, 121, 124, 128, 146, 161
saleable, 146
Sales, 46
sales, 4, 10, 16, 22, 23, 29, 35, 36, 38, 40, 48, 51, 70, 74, 77, 79, 85, 86, 88, 90, 91, 94, 99, 105, 109, 112, 119, 121, 136, 139, 141, 142, 143, 146, 150, 151, 152, 153, 154, 164, 165, 168, 173
salesman, 16, 146
salivate, 146
salty, 146
salvation, 3
same, 92, 115, 119, 146
sample, 66, 78, 94, 129, 146
samples, 66, 146
sandy, 146
sanitary, 146

sassy, 146
satisfaction, 42, 71, 86, 94, 125, 146, 164
satisfactory, 146
satisfied, 27, 37, 85, 146
satisfy, 146
satisfying, 146
saturation, 105
savable, 146
save, 146
saved, 23
saver, 168
saves, 146
saving, 56, 98, 100, 108, 146, 163
savings, 57, 98, 160
savor, 146
savvy, 106, 146
saw, 12, 84
sawed, 146
say, 19, 78, 84, 112, 113, 120, 139
saying, 114, 177
says, 12
scale, 51, 67, 73, 98, 118
scaled, 146
scales, 163
scam, 114, 115, 116
scandal, 146
scarce, 146
scare, 146
scarf, 146
scenario, 180
scene, 20, 30, 32, 56, 90, 104, 151
scenery, 27
scenes, 27
scent, 47, 67
scented, 100, 126, 146
schedule, 35, 39, 67, 146
scheduled, 146
scheme, 36, 55, 146

slick, 150
slight, 150
slim, 150
slip, 51
slow, 150, 157, 179
slowdown, 150
sluggish, 150
smacking, 100
small, 4, 16, 78, 94, 146, 150
smaller, 150
smallest, 150
smart, 36, 40, 150, 184
smarter, 63, 101, 150, 180
smash, 150, 151
smashing, 151
smell, 151
smelling, 66, 157
smelly, 151
smile, 151
smoke, 151
smoked, 151
smoking, 151
smooth, 151
smoothed, 151
smoother, 151
smothered, 151
snake, 151
snap, 16
snappy, 104
sneak, 71, 151
sneaky, 151
so, 3, 5, 85, 101, 151, 180
soaked, 151
soapy, 151
soar, 151
soaring, 151
social, 151
sodium, 151
soft, 151

softened, 151
softest, 151
software, 54, 66, 115, 131
solar, 151
sold, 37, 40, 92, 101, 151, 177, 178
solely, 151
solid, 143, 151
solution, 30, 36, 38, 39, 54, 68, 98, 125, 128, 131, 136, 148, 150, 151, 155, 163, 179
solutions, 4, 59, 74, 132, 146
solve, 151
solved, 130, 151
solving, 151
some, 71, 151, 178, 180
someone, 177
something, 20, 50, 78, 151, 165
Son, 3
soon, 22, 37, 142
sooner, 151, 179
soothing, 151
sophisticated, 79, 152
sore, 152
sorry, 184
sorted, 152
sought, 152
sound, 42, 57, 127, 151, 152
sounding, 157
sounds, 12, 84
soupy, 152
sour, 152
Source, 1, 11
source, 12, 16, 60, 84, 99, 112, 119, 120, 136, 140
sources, 96, 109
souvenir, 125, 152
space, 18, 43, 152
spam, 152
spanning, 179

table, 48, 98, 120, 143, 168
tabulate, 160
tabulated, 160
tacky, 163
tact, 58
tactics, 28, 36, 60, 89, 91, 121, 138, 160
tag, 160
tailor, 160
tailored, 160
take, 51, 72, 81, 91, 150, 160, 176
takeover, 80
taker, 143
takes, 160, 177
taking, 185
talent, 70, 156
talented, 160, 184
talk, 99, 160
talking, 58
talks, 108
tall, 160
taller, 160
tallest, 160
tamed, 160
tamper, 160
tan, 160
tantalize, 160
tantalizing, 160
tap, 81, 140, 160
tapered, 160
target, 118, 160
targeted, 67, 70, 160
task, 5, 38, 148
tasks, 122
taste, 17, 47, 59, 62, 67, 94, 140, 160
tasteful, 160
tastes, 160
tasting, 157

taught, 92
Tax, 46
tax, 19, 87, 160
teach, 85
teacher, 130
team, 47, 105, 160
tearjerker, 160
tech, 79, 87
technical, 115, 132, 160
technique, 16, 71, 89, 114, 154, 162
techniques, 100, 107, 161, 164, 168
technology, 86, 98, 128, 160
teeth, 150, 160
telephone, 66
tell, 5, 81, 84, 85, 99, 177
tempered, 80, 136
temptation, 91
tempting, 161
tender, 161
tension, 79
term, 68, 101, 114, 149
terms, 37, 57, 58, 67, 70, 161
tern, 101
terrain, 20
terrific, 161
territorial, 161
territory, 37
test, 16, 28, 153, 161
tested, 17, 26, 48, 98, 104, 125, 132, 139, 147, 161, 163
testimonials, 38, 59, 72, 78, 121, 138, 161
tests, 12, 62, 143, 152, 154
text, 4
texture, 64, 151
textured, 143
th, 10, 58, 126
than, 10, 28, 62, 65, 84, 87, 92, 98, 108, 132